GOD-GIVEN PROMISES— MEET EVERY NEED

NORMAN TAYLOR

by Joy Drummond's Dad

William Carey Library

Copyright 1981 by Norman Taylor

All Rights Reserved

No part of this book may be used or reproduced in any manner whatsoever without written permission, except in the case of brief quotations embodied in critical articles and reviews.

The publisher is pleased to present this book which has been prepared from an author-edited camera-ready copy.

All Biblical references in this book are from the Authorized (King James) Version unless otherwise indicated.

ISBN 0-87808-192-5
LC# 82-061861

First Printing, 1982
Second Printing, 1986
Third Printing, 1989

Published by
William Carey Library
1705 N. Sierra Bonita Ave.
Pasadena, California 91104

Cover Art: Carol Anderson Fuller
Printed by Patterson Printing, Michigan

PRINTED IN THE UNITED STATES OF AMERICA

This book is lovingly dedicated
to the memory of

Geraldine Ely Taylor

Who shared forty-five years of my ministry
and, with me, claimed
the many Bible promises mentioned in this book;
and, in a special way, to the memory of

Eleanor Hammond Taylor,

who encouraged me to write this narrative;
patiently reading and editing the revisions
of the manuscript; constantly praying that
the reading of this book would encourage
others to claim Bible promises and discover
for themselves how personal, living and real
her Lord could become as a result.

ACKNOWLEDGMENTS

    I wish to acknowledge with sincere appreciation the help given in various ways by Dr. W. M. Wysham and Mr. David Fulton in the preparation of this manuscript.
    Also, I am very grateful to Robin Leigh-Pemberton, Esq., of London, England, for permission to use, as an illustration, a photograph of a composite-painting which his father had prepared of our encounter with the Red Baron on February 5th, 1918.

CONTENTS

Foreword vii

Preface ix

Introduction xii

1. THE RED BARON FAILED 1
2. WAS IT LUCK OR THE LORD? 11
3. THE REASON REVEALED 21
4. PROMISED PROTECTION PROVIDED 29
5. A CHILD'S SILENCE SPOKE VOLUMES 43
6. FAITH IS BETTER THAN SIGHT 49
7. A FANTASTIC FULFILLMENT 55
8. TOO GOOD TO BE TRUE 61
9. BETTER THAN EXPECTED 69
10. ADVENTURING WITH GOD 77
11. ONE OF THE LEAST 84

12.	OTHERS JOIN IN THE ADVENTURE	90
13.	A WAY IN THE WILDERNESS	100
14.	STREAMS IN THE DESERT	107
15.	DISAPPOINTMENT OR HIS APPOINTMENT?	121
16.	SUNSET GLOW	131

Help for Daily Living: A classified index of promises mentioned in this book and others used under varied circumstances. 134

FOREWORD

Norman Taylor's work in Mexico was unique. What a tremendous difference between dropping bombs on the Kaiser's troops and planting life-giving seed in the hearts of Mexican soldiers! This book tells how some fifteen years after the First World War a former captain of the Royal Air Force, Norman Taylor, carried on this very unique ministry of seed-sowing among the military of Mexico. In gratitude to God for His protection throughout the war he had dedicated his life to God and with his wife, Geraldine, had served as missionaries in Mexico City. In fact, they were very helpful there when our pioneer Bible translation movement was being born in an Aztec village sixty-five miles away.

It was in this Indian village where the President of Mexico, General Lazaro Cardenas, first met the Taylors. The subsequent meeting which Norman tells about occured a few years later in Lower California when the remarkable general, who had completed his presidential term in 1940, had been assigned to head up the defense of Mexico's Pacific coastline against possible Japanese attacks during World War II.

I myself am a witness of the general's satisfaction over the distribution of Scriptures among the armed forces of his beloved fatherland. In fact, he decided at one point that he himself would so some distributing. Accordingly, he asked me for two hundred copies of the Spanish New Testament. Thrilled, of course, I lost no time in getting them to him. A few days later a colonel told me, "I simply have to read the Bible now, for General Cardenas sent me a copy. You can be sure that he will ask me one of these days if I have read it. So I must do so."

vii

I expect to see in glory many of the recipients of the seed sown by Cardenas, for God's Word does not return unto Him void (Isaiah 55:11). The large number of redeemed souls before the throne (Revelation 7:9) will also include many as a result of Taylor's distribution, told about in this book, which will be a cause for even greater joy.

W. Cameron Townsend, Founder
Wycliffe Bible Translators

PREFACE

On August 6th, 1985, Norman Taylor celebrated his ninety-third birthday. Living in pleasant surroundings, blessed with four children, five step-children, twenty-four grandchildren, even some great grand-children, and a host of friends, co-workers and fellow followers of our Lord, he moves toward the middle of his tenth decade. As he enjoys his well-earned retirement, his mind and spirit still range across the world into which God called him to be in mission for Jesus Christ. This second edition of his account of the first twenty-six years of his service in Latin America as a Presbyterian missionary is a sign, one among many, to those who know and love him, of his continued vigor, enthusiasm, and faithfulness to his Lord.
    This narrative focuses on the faithfulness of God and the promises of Scripture as they were claimed in a time of great change and upheaval in Mexico and Latin America. The Rev. Dr. Norman Taylor served in Mexico as an evangelist and missionary, then as chair of the Latin American Council (made up of all our representatives in Latin America), then as Secretary for Evangelism for Latin America. He retired from the cross-cultural mission field in 1959, and served as interim and associate pastor in several churches in Florida, Texas, and California, until he was well past eighty.
    However, he has never retired from his active engagement with what God is doing in this world, and through the Church. By his conversation, correspondence, reading, writing and praying, Dr. Taylor is still alert to the moving of God's Spirit around the globe. He has revised and is offering for

reprinting a third edition of *God-Given Promises - Meet Every Need*, because of the response he has had from those who read the first two editions: students, seminarians, evangelists, and those interested in cross-cultural mission.

Shortly after Dr. Taylor moved to California, his first wife, Geraldine, mother of their four children and partner in mission work for all those thirty-six years, died after a long period of suffering from emphysema. In 1968 he married Eleanor Hammond, who with her husband George had served as missionaries with the Taylors in the 1920's. A widow for ten years at the time of her marriage, Eleanor Hammond Taylor encouraged Norman to write of his faith in the promises of God, and the experience of that faith resulting in the fulfillment of those promises.

Eleanor Hammond Taylor herself died in January of 1981, before this manuscript first came into print, but not before she had enjoyed the providence of God completing a cycle in her life. In May of 1980, she returned to the Fort Street Presbyterian Church in Detroit, Michigan, where she had been married fifty-six years before, and from which as a young bride she had left with her husband George for Mexico to be Presbyterian missionaries. There, sitting in the very pew in which her parents had sat when she was married, she heard her youngest son preach to the 192nd General Assembly of the United Presbyterian Church as its Moderator. This son bears the name of a third of those missionaries to Mexico, the late Dr. Charles Ainley, remembered by many for his work in helping begin Theological Education by Extension, in Guatemala in the 1950's. God surprises us with gifts we cannot even think of requesting. The grace of God far surpasses even our imagination.

Norman Taylor tells the story of his experiences of God's grace because he has been surprised and remarkably graced with the promises of God fulfilled. He still expects them to continue to be fulfilled. So this narrative is part of a further promise, the one given to us in Acts 1, "You shall be my witnesses, in Jerusalem, and in all Judea and Samaria, and to the end of the earth...." Through this record of one man's life, others may hear the witness, and it may move through the written word of a lived life and become a living witness to the one Living Word for us all. This is one more promise that Norman Taylor claims. To his last day with us and his first day in the eternal kingdom, he will continue to seek to be one of those witnesses to the end of the earth.

This is a time of great change and upheaval in Latin America. Again, we hear most exciting records of the church, the growth of the evangelical church and the renewal of the old church. New insights into the Gospel are brought forth,

Preface

new experiments in Christian living in community, new forms of ecclesial life are acted out. Some of these will last and help reform and renew the church in the world, some will wither as of no long lasting help, but the Spirit of God still moves in that world where Norman Taylor, over sixty years ago, began to tell others what had happened in his life and could happen in theirs.

David Barrett posits sixty million Christians in Latin America in 1900, but over 392,000,000 in 1986 and estimates that by the year 2000 it will be the continent with the most Christians of any - over 500,000,000.* Norman Taylor has been an active part of making that happen.

This book gives flesh and blood to those numbers. It shows how the evangelical presence in Mexico could increase from around 60,000 in 1900, but over two million today. It happens because men and women such as Norman and Geraldine Taylor, Vera and Charles Ainley, Eleanor and George Hammond, along with an unnumbered host of others, from within and without the ancient land of Mexico, claimed God's promises. It happened as one thirsty person told another where to find the living water.

I hope as you get caught up in the excitement of this vivid story, you will find that excitement a part of your own life as you begin to live on the same principle that Norman Taylor lives, that God gives us promises in Scripture, and these promises fill our every need.

Charles Ainley Hammond
West Lafayette, Indiana
January, 1986

**International Bulletin of Missionary Research*, Vol. 10, No. 1, p. 23, 1986.

INTRODUCTION

In the First World War the Red Baron tried to send me to kingdom come. Instead he started me on a life-long quest. It was the same quest that took the patriarchs from their homeland on journeys that covered three generations. With their camels and livestock, they travelled slowly toward the destination that beckoned them on. Clouds of dust enveloped them as they crossed burning deserts. The sweat, dried in mud-globlets on their faces, also soaked their garments, as they pressed on to the next oasis. There in the fresh water they bathed, washed their clothes and their *burnous* (head cloths), rested their flocks and herds - only, after a time, to press on again.

The early Christians endured without complaint the dank darkness of the catacombs; the leg and wrist irons in the Roman gaols, for the same reason. It enabled the Apostle Paul and the Church fathers to face persecution, suffering and even death. It gave Martin Luther the assurance to wait patiently for the decision of the Diet of Augsburg. It caused Wesley, David Livingstone and countless others to cross oceans, travel over trackless plains, and through impenetrable forests, completely forgetful of themselves.

What was it that lured men, over the centuries, to exchange homes and material comforts for untold hardships and suffering? It was their faith and confidence in the reality of the promises of the Living God. For the patriarchs it was God's promise of a new homeland. For others it was the promises of His Presence: His love and blessing.

Of Martin Luther it was said that, as he prayed, he pleaded God's promises in the Psalms like one who knew that all things for which he asked would surely come to pass. He and all the others were not disappointed, because God has filled His Word with promises to meet every need in life.

As related in chapter one, my encounter with the Red Baron brought such a promise to my attention in an unforgettable manner. This made me look for other promises in the Bible to meet problems or emergencies. They created a feeling of expectancy as I watched to see where and how God would work. Soon I began to mark in the margin of my Bible the date the promise was claimed, the reason, and the results. To my amazement, God ceased to be someone far off and impersonal. He became living and real, ever present and interested in all the details of life. Life became an adventure with Him. Today these notes in the margins bring to mind experiences of God's goodness which otherwise might have been long since forgotten.

This book is a record of how faithfully God has fulfilled His promises claimed under varied and often trying circumstances.

"How happy I am because of your promises---
As happy as someone who finds rich treasure."
Psalm 119:162 (TEV)

OUR ENCOUNTER WITH THE RED BARON, FEBRUARY 5, 1918.
(A composite-painting)

1

THE RED BARON FAILED

"It is so great that you are back!" shouted our good friend Scotty Noel as we drove up to the quarters of A-Flight of 20th Squadron in France. "I was very much afraid that you might not get back in time for the big show!"

"What do you mean?" we asked almost in unison. "What has happened since we went to England?" Douglas and I had been away for about two weeks attending a special training course. It was mid-January of 1918.

"Have not the papers been reporting it?" Scotty asked in surprise.

"Reporting what?" we both exclaimed.

"The big German air offensive!"

"NO-O-O!" was our answer. "Tell us what has happened."

"The situation has changed radically. The Germans have begun an offensive all along the line to break our control of the air. They are attacking with tremendous air power and the attack is being led by the Red Knight, Baron Manfred Von Richthofen. Our turn will come soon," Scotty continued.

"The Red Baron!" exclaimed Douglas. "Every R.A.F. flier will welcome the chance to tangle with him. May it come soon."

"Right!" answered Scotty. "But let's not forget that this may well be the prelude to a massive ground offensive by the Germans all along the northern sector of the Allies' front line."

The next few days brought further news of continued attacks by the Red Baron and his squadrons on narrow sectors of the line. Unfortunately, there were reports also of very heavy casualties among our fliers.

On February 5, 1918, Douglas and I were on a regular patrol with twelve or fifteen other planes when suddenly, out of the clouds, there appeared about three times that number of German planes. There seemed to be three squadrons. One group of planes was painted in a black and white checkerboard pattern. Another had blue fuselages and yellow wings, while the third was the dreaded Red Squadron of the Red Baron.

In the midst of the dogfight which followed, my gun jammed and Douglas climbed out of the fray to an altitude of over 19,000 feet while I struggled to fix the gun. In those early days no oxygen was carried and I remember gasping for breath in the rarefied air as I tried to make the repairs. It seemed like ages, but was probably only a few minutes before the gun was working again and we dropped down into the fight.

Douglas saw one of our planes with several Germans attacking it and went to its assistance. In a moment five planes were attacking us from above and below. Completely outnumbered, we did not have a chance, so Douglas put the nose down, side-slipping one way and another as we lost altitude, to let me handle them from the rear.

Each time a bullet hit our plane we felt it quiver. After I had fired first at one and then at another, somehow four of the planes disappeared. But one enemy plane stayed under our tail, in spite of Douglas' skillful handling of our aircraft, and I could see his tracer bullets coming closer and closer to our cockpits. I recognized that the end was inevitable, took a chance and shot very close to our tail. I could have shot away our controls. The enemy plane veered upward and then headed for the ground.

We were alone and badly shaken, but a glance showed that the plane was also in very bad shape. Something was wrong with the engine and one wing seemed loose. It was a long way back to the airfield, so we were horrified when the engine died. Every foot possible was squeezed from our altitude as we glided westward. The airfield came in sight. Could we possibly make it? Gliding over the tree tops and between them, we finally reached the far end of our large airfield, and made a safe landing.

The Bristol Fighter was a two-seater single engine, high flying biplane, and was almost as maneuverable as a single-seat scout. The new model, which we were flying, had been introduced only recently and was still considered one of the most effective planes in the air. It had two open cockpits. The pilot had two guns that were synchronized to fire through the propeller. The observer sat facing the tail of the plane and had a machine gun mounted on a rack that ran on a track, encircling the cockpit. This enabled him to swing his gun and fire in almost any direction. The plane also had a makeshift dual control, giving the observer a slight chance of guiding the plane down, should his pilot be killed or wounded. In those early days no parachutes were carried by fliers.

While we waited for mechanics to arrive, we took stock of our plane. The crankcase of the engine had been shot through causing the oil to drain out. We were surprised that it had run for some minutes, giving us a good start for the airfield. The magneto at Douglas' side had been hit. There was a bullet hole in the sleeve of my flying coat, another in my heavy boots, and in the fabric of the plane there were fifty-two bullet holes.

The mechanics arrived and, tearing off the fabric, found that four main spars had been chipped or shot through and other damage to the structure of the plane.

"By all the rules of the game, Captain," one of the mechanics said as he turned to me, "you should have broken up in the air. I don't know what held your plane together."

Immediately there came to my mind a Bible promise that my sister Muriel had claimed for me when in early 1917 I had decided to transfer from the Canadian Forces in France to the Royal Flying Corps, which later became knows as the Royal Air Force. She had written, "As I pray for you I am claiming the promise, 'The eternal God is thy refuge, and underneath are the everlasting arms.'" (Deut. 33:27)

"The everlasting arms must have been underneath us today," I thought, as I looked at the splintered spars and the bullet-ridden wings. "If not, we would have gone to pieces in the air as others have."

The question kept coming to mind: Why had God brought us through safely? Did He have some purpose in all this? I could not accept the comments of our companions, "You are just plain lucky!" or "Where do you keep your horse-shoes?"

I had grown up in a Christian home and, as a boy, had been a regular attendant at Sunday school and church. In later adolescence I stopped attending and so had reached manhood without making any meaningful commitment to Christ. I knew I should do so, but because of a wrong concept of the nature of God, I was reluctant to put my life in His hands. To do so, it seemed to me, would mean missing the best things of life.

In the summer of 1914 a friend, Pace Thompson, and I spent our vacation tracing the old historic Dawson Trail in western Ontario. It began at the western end of Lake Superior and, before the railroads were built, was the only route in Canada by which the West and the Yukon could be reached. On lakes and rivers, the principal means of transportation was the old York Boat, a flat-bottomed, simple-to-construct craft. Some were powered by steam engines. It was a fascinating trip. In the clear waters of the lakes we could see the remains of these boats where they had rotted and sunk at their moorings, when no longer needed as a means of transportation.

One day we stopped at an Indian trading post to replenish our supplies. The trader wrapped our things in old newspapers. In our canoe we returned to our camp and began to transfer our supplies into waterproof bags. As we unwrapped each package, some news item would catch our eyes and we would read it aloud. We had been out of touch with the world for several weeks and were eager for news. As I opened one parcel and saw the headlines, I was left speechless. It was hard to believe my eyes! All I could do was hold it out for Pace to see and exclaim, "Look!"

WAR DECLARED ON GERMANY. CANADA JOINS ALLIES. It was the front page of the Winnipeg Free Press for August 4, 1914.

"It isn't possible!" he exclaimed, and we both huddled over the sheet to read the details. All packing stopped as we read and reread the astounding news.

Around our campfire, late into the night, we talked about what this might mean to each one of us. Pace was in the midst of a law course. Should he quit and enlist? We finally decided we should return home as quickly as possible and join the army. It was well that we could not see the future. For me it was to be a life-changing experience. For Pace--six feet of ground in France in September of 1918.

When we reached home a week later, we found that the First Contingent had been formed already. We volunteered for the Second, which was to be called up in the fall.

Reports of heavy casualties in France made me think more seriously about spiritual matters, but without coming to any definite decision. The evening before I was to report for service, I drove my sister Muriel to an orphanage where she was to give a message to the children. She spoke about Christ as "The Good Shepherd" and explained how loving and kind God is. He always seeks the best for those who trust Him, and will bring into their lives a peace and joy that can be found in no other way. Suddenly it dawned on me how mistaken I had been about Him and I was ashamed of my doubts and unwillingness to trust Him. When Muriel gave an invitation to the children to open their hearts to Christ and invited them to come forward, I went with the children and almost broke up the meeting. For years Muriel and my mother had been praying that I might make this decision.

The Red Baron Failed

The next day I reported for overseas service. Army training followed and early summer of 1915 found us on a transport bound for England. After a few more months of training, we were sent to France as reinforcements to the First Canadian Division.

Entering the army immediately after my conversion gave little opportunity for me to learn about the Christian Life; the need for Bible study, prayer and our responsibility to witness. Soon my life was little different from those about me, except that God kept me from the moral excesses of some.

There is no doubt in my mind that Christ came into my heart that night at the orphanage. I took His salvation but gave little of myself in return and so did not have the peace and joy which could have been mine. I knew that something vital was missing but had no one near at hand to whom I could go for advice. We were kept so busy that there was little time for reading or meditation and during our training period the religious services were rather perfunctory. In France our detail rarely saw a chaplain.

Normally I had a rather happy disposition and could not understand why I should feel so miserable and frustrated. I was so ignorant about the Christian Life that I did not recognize that I was under conviction for my failure to do the necessary things to nurture my spirit and cause it to grow. Then there came a personal experience that forced me to recognize that God was present and working in my life.

Our camp was moved into a new area in France, right next to a British naval airfield. The squadron was flying the new triplanes which were supposed to be something unique. The science of aeronautics was in its infancy and it was thought that by adding another wing on top, the plane ought to be able to climb more rapidly and carry an additional load. At first opportunity I visited the naval airfield.

On this visit I discovered that an old school friend was one of the pilots. My admiration for all flyers was extreme and I wanted to find out all I could about the service, so I invited Bob McNeil to have dinner with us the following day. The others in our mess were not as interested in flying as I, and so after dinner we returned to my tent and the conversation naturally turned to old times and old friends.

In the midst of our conversation suddenly a voice, which I knew was not audible, said to me, "Speak to him about salvation. Speak to him about his soul." It startled and amazed me! What was it? Who was it? I found myself without the ready knowledge nor the courage to speak to Bob about Christ. He must have sensed my preoccupation, for in a few minutes he excused himself and returned to the airfield. As we parted he called back, "I'll see you at dinner the day after tomorrow," reminding me of his return invitation.

The following afternoon, as I rode into our lines, I saw in the distance the triplanes returning from patrol. Suddenly one of them disintegrated in the air and the fuselage plummeted to the ground. The six wings floated earthward in its wake. I was still on my horse and for a moment I considered riding the mile or more to the site of the crash, but recalled a pressing duty and dismounted.

I had seen other planes crash and had come to think of them in an impersonal way. In flying I found that this was common among most men. An enemy plane was a machine to be destroyed and one did not think of the occupant. A callousness had developed, perhaps consciously, to enable us to perform a duty which was unavoidable. That afternoon it did not occur to me to wonder whose plane had gone to pieces in the air.

The next evening I went over to the airfield in response to Bob's invitation, and meeting an officer inquired, "Where will I find Bob McNeil's tent?"

He gave me a startled look and after a pause responded, "Didn't you know that yesterday afternoon Bob's plane went to pieces in the air and he was instantly killed?"

In a daze I returned to my tent and had a period of soul searching. Why hadn't I said something? I could have told him my own experience. Why did I remain silent? After further thought I had to recognize that what had silenced me was pride. I admired fliers and wanted to be one and did not want Bob to think of me as a "religious nut." Then self was more important to me than Christ! I had failed both God and my friend and I loathed myself for my cowardice! At that moment I tried to put the whole matter out of my mind but was unsuccessful. It kept haunting me and with the memory of a lost opportunity came more self-condemnation.

I sought God's forgiveness repeatedly and found temporary relief but it soon was lost in a return of self-condemnation. I could not forgive myself for my failure to witness to my friend. Mistakenly I began to think there was virtue in this self-judgment and there developed a false sense of rightness in my self-condemnation. The result was an increasing indifference toward spiritual matters.

Some time had to pass before it began to dawn on me that by continuing to condemn myself I was failing to accept the forgiveness I sought from God. To truly experience God's forgiveness for my failures I must be willing to forgive myself. This was confirmed to me by a study of I John 1:9, "If we confess our sins, He is faithful and just to forgive us our sins, and to cleanse us from all unrighteousness." God promises to forgive and to forget our sins and failures by cleansing us, making it possible to begin again with a clear conscience. When this important truth was seen and appropriated, I experienced peace on the matter and a renewed desire to have fellowship with the Lord.

By early 1917 I had become sick and tired of the muck and mud of a stalemated war and when there appeared in General Orders an invitation for officers who had seen service in France to transfer to the Royal Flying Corps, I sent in my application. Some weeks passed, but finally it came through and I returned to England for training. Then I learned that we were not to be trained as pilots but as observers. Today we call them gunners.

The Flying Corps had suffered very heavy casualties and by getting officers from France the training period could be reduced to a minimum. It was! Our training included a brush-up on the use of a machine gun, something on map reading and observation but, although the planes had makeshift dual control, no instruction was given on how to fly the plane in case of an emergency. A ten day leave was given when the training was completed and within less than thirty days, I was back in France again as a reinforcement to the 20th Squadron of Bristol Fighters. The squadron was located in northern France near the Belgian border.

Reporting at the squadron headquarters, I learned that pilot reinforcements were expected within a few days and I would be assigned to fly with one of the new men. We were only "seconded" or loaned to the airforce, continuing to wear our old uniforms and keep the rank we had in our former unit. I had become a captain in the Canadian forces and, since I had higher rank than most of the other reinforcements, the commanding officer told me that I could choose the pilot with whom I wished to fly.

A few days later the new pilots arrived and immediately were sent up to demonstrate their flying ability. Sandbags were put in the observers' cockpit. Each flyer was supposed to bring his plane down at a designated spot and make a "three point" landing, that is to say, the wheels and the tail skid were to touch the ground simultaneously. This was important because in those early days the planes had no brakes and were stopped by the tail skid scraping along the ground. Each took his turn as we watched critically, realizing that our lives might depend upon the pilot's skill. None made perfect landings.

Then came one who, failing to make a perfect landing, took off again. He came in for another landing, but again the tail skid did not touch down as it should, and he took off for the third try. By this time everyone was joking, "His gas will run out and he will have to stay down." But I thought differently! Here was a man who is determined to make a perfect landing regardless of how he might be laughed at. The third try was perfect and the plane stopped quickly. I turned to the commanding officer and said, "If that man is willing, I would like to fly with him."

This was my introduction to Douglas Leigh-Pemberton. He was an officer in the famous British regiment, the Grenadier Guards. It is the unit which guards Buckingham Palace. He had already seen many months of service in France with his own regiment before transferring to the Royal Air Force. As was shown clearly by his determination to make a perfect landing on his trial flight, he was a disciplined man and soon became an accomplished pilot. Also, I found him to be a delightful companion. We both enjoyed outdoor sports and on days when flying was impossible we explored the countryside on horses he was able to borrow from friends on the headquarters staff.

Soon after we began flying together, I mentioned that in my training no instruction had been given in the use of the dual control system with which our plane was equipped.

"What!" he exclaimed. "They gave you no instruction on how to fly the plane?"

"Yes, that's a fact! I guess they were too short of observers in France to take the time. All our instruction lasted less than three weeks."

"I recognize that this dual control system is very inadequate," Douglas continued. "You have no control of the ailerons, can only move the rudder by grabbing the cable that goes through your cockpit, but it is the only chance you observers have, if the pilot is killed or badly wounded. From now on, when we get on our side of the line, you are going to fly us home."

"Okay. That will be fine, but I won't try landing on our field. There is too much traffic."

"Somewhere we will find an uncluttered place where you can practice," Douglas replied. "It is vitally important that you learn."

The first few months were routine--early morning patrols and one or two more during the day. As a high flying fighting squadron, our task was to intercept the German planes as they climbed for altitude before attacking our observation planes, flying at about four thousand feet along the battle line. To accomplish this, we flew at a high altitude and about fifty miles inside the German-held

The Red Baron Failed

territory. An occasional dogfight broke the monotony of these patrols.

The higher command, recognizing the dullness of this daily routine, began organizing shooting competitions between squadrons. These were held at the coast, over the English Channel. Just before Christmas 1917, Douglas and I were sent to represent our squadron at one. It was held at Berck-Sur-Mer on the coast. After we had identified the spot, Douglas turned the plane toward the Channel and as we flew along the towering cliffs, he called, "Look down!" As I did, I saw the wide beaches that spread out at the base of the cliffs.

"There is where you can practice landing," he shouted over his shoulder.

"It's an ideal spot," I shouted back. "No planes landing or taking off to avoid."

"Perhaps there will be time after the contest. We will find out our schedule and make plans."

For two days most of the daylight hours were spent waiting to go up and shoot at a variety of targets which were towed behind a plane. When we had taken our final turn, we headed for the beach, not bothering to come down to find out our score.

I was thrilled to be about to do what I had imagined doing so many times. Soon we were above the beach. I took over the controls. In a moment the cliffs towered above us as we neared the sand. The tail was in a good position for a three-point landing. We touched down . . . but the plane did not stop. We had forgotten that the sand would be frozen hard and so the skid could not cut into it. Now the sloping beach caused us to veer toward the breakers.

"I'll take over!" Douglas shouted and as he spoke he opened the throttle wide. We arose from the beach only yards short of the surf.

Suddenly a strong downdraft from the cliffs struck the plane and forced it down until a large wave hit the wheels and we nose-dived into the sea! I was thrown some distance from the plane, but Douglas, having a seat belt, found himself hanging head downward in the sinking plane. As soon as I came to the surface, I yanked off my flying goggles and swam toward the plane. The tide was rising rapidly, but upon reaching the plane I found I could just touch bottom. Each wave was engulfing Douglas as he struggled to free himself from the seat belt. I got one foot on a wheel strut, heaved Douglas up a little and in a moment he was free. With water to our necks, we waded ashore and in a few moments our clothes were frozen hard. The waves soon turned the plane on its back and we watched it sink under the rising tide.

We were icy cold and started running along the beach to restore our circulation. As we looked at the towering cliffs, we began to wonder where an ascent could be found. Fortunately, someone still in the air had seen us go down and soon a truck came speeding up to the beach. They took us to our quarters, which were unheated, and there was no hot water. However, a vigorous rubdown helped and by going to bed fully dressed, including our overcoats, we got our teeth to stop chattering. Next day we were none the worse for our experience.

The mechanics went to the scene of our crash when the tide was out and dragged the plane up on the beach. It was found to be completely useless. Sea water had soaked the plane, engine and all the instruments. When we learned this, we began to wonder what disciplinary action might be taken against us for having foolishly lost a plane. The next day, which was December 24, we drove back to our squadron and waited rather tensely for a call from the commanding officer. Christmas passed without a summons to the Orderly Room. Early next day it came! Two rather contrite young men presented themselves at the appointed hour. As we entered the office, the major arose from his desk and came to meet us.

"My sincere congratulations on the excellent score you made in the competition. Our squadron had one of the highest records!" he announced while we remained speechless from surprise. We still had not found our voices when he continued, "Just this morning orders have come for me to send two officers to England for some kind of special course. They give no details. I have chosen you two. Be ready to leave in the morning."

We could not believe our ears! We must be dreaming! Next day we knew it was not a dream because we were enroute for the Port of Bologne and then England. But for what kind of a course?

2

WAS IT LUCK OR THE LORD?

"Taylor and Pemberton of 20th Squadron reporting for the special course which is to begin tomorrow," said Douglas to an officer in the Air Ministry, whom we had located with some difficulty.

"A bus will be leaving at four this afternoon from the courtyard," he said without looking up from his desk. "You can leave your kit-bags in the guard house."

"Thank you, sir!" we replied in unison and turned to leave.

"You said 20th Squadron?" he inquired almost absent-mindedly.

"Yes, sir!" I replied, and then inquired, "May I ask, sir, what is the nature of the course we are to take?"

"Oh, just the usual things," he replied, still without looking up from his desk. The reason for our coming to England continued to be a mystery.

The bus took us to an airdrome in Surrey and, that evening after dinner, a colonel briefed us on the purpose of our coming.

"We welcome you to the first course of instruction that has ever been given on a new invention which we believe will revolutionize aerial warfare. It is still a military secret and we want you to be careful with whom you discuss what you learn here." Then he went on to explain that we were to study the wireless telephone, which we today call radio.

"Tomorrow morning," the colonel continued, "you will be at our airfield at eight o'clock and report to Major Victor

Tate. He will conduct a demonstration so that you can all see the great possibilities of this new invention."

"Vic Tate!" The name rang a bell. "Could this man be the friend of my brother Colin? He is an electrical engineer," I remembered, and as soon as the session was over I sought him out and found that he was the same man. It was good to see someone from home.

Early next morning an excited group of officers gathered on the airfield. We found that there were only six or seven planes equipped with the new apparatus, one with the sending equipment and the others equipped to receive the message. This meant that we would have to fly in several groups.

"As you have seen," said Major Tate, "the planes you will fly are equipped with receiving equipment. There are two sets of headphones but the dials for tuning in are in the observer's cockpit. You will climb to 5,000 feet in formation, then tune in to my signal. When we are in contact, fire a colored light. Since you have to take turns in flying, I have divided up the group as follows."

To our great delight Douglas and I were in the first group to go up. Soon we were at the proper altitude and began to tune in. Colored lights were fired and we looked expectantly toward the speck in the distance which was Major Tate's plane.

"Hello, Norm," suddenly came over the air and I recognized Vic's voice. "How would you like to be at the corner of Portage Avenue and Main Street right now?"

It seemed incredible! Utterly impossible! Was I dreaming this? Yet I recognized his voice and there flashed into my mind a picture of the familiar corner in our home city. The next few minutes were too busy to think about this experience. First the whole group was ordered to do certain things in formation. Then individual planes were ordered to leave the formation, as would be the case if specific targets were to be bombed. Finally we were ordered to descend to the field, but even as we dropped down Major Tate continued to speak to us about the great change we could expect in our flying routine.

The next group, taking our places in the planes, took off. Major Tate remained in the air and we watched with interest as the colored lights appeared and the group was put through the same tactics we had just completed. Finally, just one group remained to have its turn. As the planes landed and the remaining men took their places in them, to our surprise Major Tate's plane taxied to where we all were standing.

Was It Luck or the Lord?

"Norm," he called, "you and Douglas take this plane up and do for these men what I've been doing. I have to be ready for a class when you all come down."

We could hardly believe our good luck, but jumped into his plane and he gave me a few extra instructions about how to manipulate the dials. In a few minutes we were all at the proper altitude and I began to give the prearranged signal. Soon the lights were going up from the formation, which we could hardly see in the distance. Putting them through the proper tactics was no problem and it was soon over. Suddenly my sense of humor got the best of me and I called over the telephone, "As you guys return to the field, I'll entertain you with the best of music!" And I began to sing "Tipperary," "Keep the Home Fires Burning," and snatches of other familiar songs.

The group reached the airfield before we did and as I climbed out of the plane, I received a lot of good-humored comments about my singing. None of them was especially complimentary, but we all had a good laugh from the thought of "flying to music"! I may not have been the first person to sing over the radio, but I am sure I can claim the doubtful honor of having broadcasted to the smallest audience--twelve men, and some of them may well have tuned me out before they reached the ground!

It had been a most exciting day and that night I found it hard to go to sleep. As I lay there mulling over the events of the day, there came to mind a disturbing thought that kept me awake for a long while.

"If man can make an apparatus that without wires, and while we were high in the air, could bring Vic's voice to me so clearly that I could recognize it, why do I doubt that God can hear prayer?" As I lay there trying to analyze my doubts and find some reasonable excuse for my failure to pray, there came to mind an experience I had when a little boy. In almost an amusing way, I had discovered that God did hear and answer prayer.

Our home in Winnipeg was situated on the Assiniboine River. Steep willow-covered banks led down to the rather muddy stream, which was a source of all kinds of pleasures. The steep banks made an ideal toboggan slide in the winter and summer brought boating and fishing.

One day, when I was about seven years old, I had spent an hour or more fishing in the river without success. Then there came to mind a recent Sunday school lesson on prayer. Mr. Moore, our teacher, had said that God loved to answer prayer. There, sitting on the muddy river bank watching the "tell-tale stick" to which my line was tied, the thought came that perhaps God would hear a prayer for some fish.

Why not try it? So, with one eye half open to watch the mud-ball which topped the stick, I prayed. It was not the child's prayer said each night, but direct and to the point. After all, one could not keep his eyes closed for long when watching a fishing line. "Dear Lord, please give me some fish," was the gist of my prayer. I had hardly opened my eyes when the mud-ball fell off the stick, and soon a big silver goldeye lay on the river bank beside me. Excitedly, I baited the hook and threw in the line again. In a few minutes there was another jerk on the line and soon a second goldeye lay beside the first. This continued until six lovely fish had been landed. A very proud little boy strung them on a cord and carried them triumphantly to his mother. No one could convince him that God did not answer prayer. He knew that He did!

What had happened to the faith of my childhood?

Again I thought over the events of the day. The whole thing still seemed incredible, but I knew that the experiences were real. As long as we were tuned in, Vic's voice had followed us. We heard him in the air and on the ground when we landed. Could God hear our prayers with equal ease? Would He hear us from anywhere? Would a prayer from a trench or aircraft be heard by God as readily as one coming from inside a church? As I asked the question, the answer was plain. Then why had I stopped praying? Someone had told us that a thing called "static" could make communication difficult on the wireless telephone.

"Lord, is there such a thing as spiritual static?" I prayed. I went to sleep with the question unanswered, but without realizing it I had begun to pray again spontaneously.

The next few days were long and busy but extremely interesting as we studied the wireless telephone. Because of the analogy which had come to me between prayer and the wireless telephone, I listened with special interest when static or broken contacts were discussed. It seemed that a faulty generator or even a loose electrical connection could cause trouble. Little details were very important.

The course ended and we all returned to our squadrons in France. It had been a thrilling experience, but our elation had been subdued the last night when the colonel, in answer to a question from one of our group, had informed us, "It will probably be the end of May or June before we can begin to equip the planes in France with this new invention."

"May or June, sir!" the officer replied. "We will all be killed or invalided home before that date!"

Many of us were sorry the question had been asked, although it was in all our minds. The officer's prediction proved largely true, for I am sure that few of us who took that first course ever used the wireless telephone in combat.

Soon after our return to France came our encounter with the Red Baron, which is related in the first chapter, and the remarkable fulfillment of the promise, "Underneath are the everlasting arms," that my sister had claimed for me in prayer. It strengthened my faith in prayer . . . but it was still faith that God would answer the prayers of others, rather than mine.

The Red Baron's air offensive caused heavy casualties in our squadron and this was followed by an unfortunate automobile accident which put more of our men in the hospital. Our A-Flight was reduced to five pilots and four observers. The orders were that the pilots could take turns flying, but Douglas went to our commanding officer and asked to be allowed to fly with me on all the missions, recognizing that changing partners could be very dangerous. I was very grateful to him for this courageous act. Fortunately, the next week or two were very quiet on our sector of the line and soon our A-Flight was back to full strength.

Believing that the all-out attack against our air force had seriously crippled it, about the middle of March, 1918, the Germans launched a tremendous ground attack against the Allied line in the Somme area of northern France. Within a few days all the territory that had been won at great cost was lost.

On March 26 we were awakened very early and told to prepare to leave within a short time. At dawn the whole squadron was to fly east to an airfield at Brouay. A number of squadrons were being concentrated at that place, to hold back the Germans from the air while the Allied ground forces prepared a new front line.

At Brouay we received orders to fly at 3,000 feet and, when over enemy territory, to break formation with each plane seeking its own ground target among the advancing Germans. We soon found a back road with troops, but they were marching in such close formation that it made identification almost impossible. We feared they might be our own troops retreating. We dropped down to 300 feet, almost above their heads, but even then their discipline was so good that not one head looked upward. If one had done so, we could have recognized the special shape of the German helmet. They came to a ruined village and two men went forward to reconnoiter. As they bent forward to look around the corner, the shape of the helmet became clear.

"They are Huns!" Douglas shouted. "There is no doubt. They are Huns! But we have to get some altitude before diving on them."

We climbed immediately and dived, dropping our load of bombs and firing as we dove. They at once took refuge in ditches and among the ruined houses. As we climbed out of each dive, I used the rear gun. There was much return fire, but we continued to dive and climb until our ammunition was exhausted.

Returning to the airfield at Brouay, we found that our plane had been hit by ground fire a number of times, and one bullet hole was through the seat in my cockpit. I must have been standing and firing over the side of the plane when it came through.

After lunch we were ordered on another patrol. As we were about to take off, our commander came out and stopped us.

"That plane is too badly damaged to fly. Change to mine."

In making the hurried change, Douglas forgot to put on his seat belt, and this oversight may well have saved his life.

We both had served in this area with the ground forces and knew it fairly well. Since we had been delayed in taking off, we chose not to overtake the squadron but to look for our own ground target. We were certain that the Germans would concentrate near the ruins of Albert. Flying there, we soon found a road filled with advancing troops. So great was their confidence that they had their transport wagons with them. We dropped our bombs, but had made only three or four dives on them when I saw gasoline pouring from our rear tank through a jagged hole. I shouted the news to Douglas.

"Our front tank is shot through, too," he called back. "We're done!"

A moment later our engine died, but in those few seconds Douglas had headed our plane westward and we began a gliding descent. We had little over a thousand feet of altitude and could not glide much more than a mile. German soldiers were already following us, running across the shell-cratered fields. Ahead we saw an area partially obscured by heavy smoke. In retreating, our troops had tried to destroy supplies and equipment and the fire had spread to the dry grass around. We tried to glide beyond the area, but our plane lost flying speed and nose-dived into the smoke. As we crashed I flung myself over my machine gun, which was pointing to the rear, and hung on. Not being strapped in, Douglas was flung clear. The plane telescoped, and the engine tore through the pilot's cockpit. I don't remember jumping out of the plane, but found myself on my feet looking for Douglas. Through the smoke I saw him lying about fifty feet away. One foot seemed to be at a right angle to his leg.

I hurried over to him, calling out, "Is your leg broken?"

"No!" he replied, to my great relief. "My flying boot has slipped off, but I think my left arm is broken." He also had some bad cuts.

I helped him get his boot on and put his broken arm in his flying coat, buttoning it up to support the arm. Cautiously we headed west through the smoke.

The wrecked plane, saturated with gasoline, must have caught fire because the German soldiers, in relentless pursuit, did not search for us in the smoking field. They must have thought we were killed in the crash. We heard their shouts beyond the pall.

As the smoke thinned, we moved forward more carefully. At one side I saw the entrance to an abandoned dugout.

"Perhaps we ought to hide here until dark," I suggested.

"No indeed!" Douglas replied emphatically. "It is now or never!"

"You're right," I agreed. "Before dark the Germans will have a new front line established. We have to get through now."

Our situation was desperate. We were in the midst of hundreds of advancing troops and German patrols were everywhere between us and the British front line. We left the burning area and, taking advantage of old trenches, bushes, and ruined houses, we hurried westward.

Suddenly we saw ahead of us a German patrol coming along a narrow gauge railway line. We dropped into a shell hole and froze, scarcely daring to breathe, and they passed so close we could hear them talking. Two or three times more we hid until patrols passed, but none came as close as the first. The sound of British guns grew louder and we took courage. We had been moving west for almost two hours.

As we ran across an open space to find more cover, a patrol in the distance spotted us and opened fire. There was no further need for concealment. We threw away our heavy flying coats and ran openly as fast as we could. I took Douglas' right arm to help him along. I was exhausted and he must have been close to collapse.

"Crack!" "Crack!" "Crack!" The bullets came in quick succession, followed by another volley. We were presenting too large a target, so we separated. More shots!

"I'm hit!" Douglas exclaimed. He stumbled and almost fell. I turned to grab him.

"It's all right!" he called. It's only my right hand." If the bullet had come a foot to the left it would have struck his leg and he would have been unable to go on.

For some reason the patrol separated. Only one man continued to follow us, but he was gaining rapidly although he had to stop frequently to fire. When it seemed our strength was completely gone, I saw two heads appear in a trench and from the shape of their helmets knew they were British Tommies. I got Douglas to an old trench and left him as I ran forward to the British front line and ordered the men to fire upon the German following us. They did, and covered me as I went out to bring Douglas in. When we got into the trench one of the men, a corporal, remarked, "You are blooming lucky, Captain. If that man had not been shooting at you and we saw the bullets were coming close, we would have shot you as you neared our line. Them's our orders. The enemy are mighty sly and try all sorts of tricks."

We were passed from one group to another until we reached Brigade headquarters, where an ambulance was called. It finally arrived and with others, we were taken to a field ambulance station where Douglas' arm was put in splints and his hand properly bandaged.

"Do you feel a little better now?" I asked Douglas, as we sat on the ground in the darkness with other walking cases.

"Yes," he replied, "the pain is much less."

There was little talking among the group. No doubt all felt exhausted, as I did, from what we had been through.

Looking up at the star-lit sky, the thought came, "We have been reported 'missing in action.' No one knows where we are--but God does! God alone!" The thought caused me to relax and doze a little. Some time during the night we reached a field hospital.

During those long hours of waiting and travelling I had time to recall the events of the day. At least four times, the Hand of God could be seen in fulfillment of His promise in Deuteronomy 33:27, of being a "Refuge." The bullet hole in the cockpit seat; crashing in a burning field so that we could get away in the smoke; being unseen by the first patrol, and finally to be seen and pursued at just the right time to save us from being shot by our own men. Each incident was a miracle in itself! As I thought on these things, I had a growing sense of awe.

It seemed that we had hardly touched the bed in the field hospital before we were awakened to board a hospital train bound for the coast. The train did not pull out until about noon, and it was several hours before were were given any food. It was most welcome, for we had not eaten in more than twenty-four hours.

About dusk we reached Etaples on the French coast and were taken to the Duchess of Westminster Hospital. Two days later, Douglas was put on a hospital ship for England and our days of flying together were over.

I was sure that we had been reported "missing in action" when we failed to return from our mission and was very anxious to cable home. Arriving at the base hospital, a chaplain very kindly cared for the matter. Providentially, my message and the official telegram from Ottawa reached Winnipeg at the same time. A very thoughtful operator, when phoning my home, read my cable first.

From the hospital I also wrote some friends in England, relating our experiences, mentioning that we had been shot down before three in the afternoon and had reached our front line after five o'clock. Their reply seemed almost unbelievable. That very afternoon they had met for prayer to remember their husbands, brothers, and sons who were in France. They also prayed for me and, feeling a special burden, continued their meeting an extra half hour. The very time we were in greatest danger!

The feeling of awe, which I sensed when reviewing God's protecting care, deepened still more. I meditated, "Why should God be so good to me when I have failed Him so often?" I could think of nothing in me or that I had done that would merit such loving treatment. As I thought on the matter, I was reminded that salvation and every other blessing are all gifts from God and not of works. All that I had experienced was simply further evidence of His grace and love.

Ten days in the hospital gave me plenty of time to think. I knew that God had answered the prayers of my family and friends. Why was it that I had confidence that God heard their prayers but felt that mine did not reach much higher than the ceiling? Recalling the prayers of these friends in England, I recognized that, when they prayed, one felt that they were speaking to someone nearby whom they knew well. There was an intimacy and reality in their words that gave even a listener the assurance that they were in communion with God. How could such an intimate relationship be established? I thought a lot on this matter. It was vital! How could God become real to me?

When I was discharged from the hospital, I returned to my squadron. However, I must have suffered more shock than the doctors had recognized. When I flew, everything was fine as we climbed, patrolled, or even had a dogfight; but when we began to descend, I became airsick, and, to use the graphic terms of that day, I "painted the tail." When I began to dream that I was flying and became ill, it reached the ears of the medical officer and I found myself in the hospital again. From there I was returned to England and after a couple of weeks in a hospital, it was decided that I should be returned to Canada to recuperate. I had been in France for over three years.

After two or three months' leave, I was to go on light duty. My sister and mother began to pray that I might be assigned to the Canadian Airforce office in Winnipeg. About the middle of September, 1918, I received orders to report for duty there. When I presented myself, the major in charge almost had a fit.

"What kind of pull do you have in Ottawa? For weeks I have been trying to get a good friend of mine appointed here. Now you appear!"

It did not seem to be the opportune moment to explain to the irate major that in this case the pull was with the Highest Authority, the One who had promised, "Call upon me and I will answer thee, and show great and mighty things which thou knowest not." (Jeremiah 33:3)

Although I had joined in praying that this appointment might be made and recognized that God had fulfilled His promise, it still seemed to me that God must have answered the prayers of others rather than my own.

3

THE REASON REVEALED

Sixty thousand people lined Main Street in Winnipeg that cold, dreary afternoon of November 3, 1918. The crowds had gathered to pay their last respects to a young man who, only a few weeks before, had been awarded the Victoria Cross by the King of England. This was the highest honor that the British Empire could bestow upon a military man for an act of bravery. Allen McLeod and his observer had been shot down and their plane crashed in "no man's land" between the British and German trenches. He carried his badly wounded companion back into our trenches and, while doing so, was hit seven times by enemy machine gun bullets.

Both were so severely wounded that it was some months before they could leave the hospital and be sent back to Canada to recuperate. Before leaving England, at a ceremony at Buckingham Palace, Allen was awarded the honor he so richly deserved. In Ottawa he was received by the governor general and arriving in Winnipeg he was met by the mayor of the city and other dignitaries. After more ceremonies he returned to his home town, near the city, only to succumb to the flue epidemic a few weeks later.

The funeral service, held in a centrally located chapel, was private. When it concluded, we carried the casket on our shoulders through the crowd for a block or more before strapping it upon a gun carriage. Then we six, who were pallbearers, marched three on each side while behind came a band playing solemn martial music. A battalion of soldiers followed. Above the sound of the band could be heard the tramp, tramp, tramp of the soldiers' steel-studded boots.

To me, shocked by the death of this friend, the sound of the marching feet seemed to be saying, "E-ter-ni-ty, e-ter-ni-ty, e-ter-ni-ty." I walked beside the gun carriage unconscious of the thousands on the streets. My mind was filled with the sudden realization of how worthless were the world's honors to Allen now that he was in the presence of the King of Kings.

As the cortege wound its way slowly to the cemetery, I determined to seek a closer relationship with God, and be done with the unsatisfactory and unsatisfying, up and down spiritual experience which had been mine. So far, in spite of many evidences of God's love and care, the peace which He had promised had not been mine and I was troubled in my heart over this condition.

In my Bible reading I came across another promise, "Then shall we know if we follow on to know the Lord." (Hosea 6:3) And my prayer was that I might learn to follow and come to know Him in a new way as a living reality.

I had been brought up in the Anglican Church (Episcopal) but had left it and so had no church relationship. Some of my family attended a Bible conference center called Elim Chapel and greatly enjoyed the many outstanding Bible teachers who came to the Chapel from time to time. I attended with them and found the speakers very helpful and inspiring, but somehow my problems were not touched in these conferences. I was acquainted with the pastor, but he had no idea of my struggles and I was ashamed to go to him and admit my failures and defeats.

Nearby there was a small Pentecostal church and although I knew nothing about them and had not attended any of their services, a friend suggested that I go to one of their meetings. She told me that they had a prayer room, and that people were there to pray with anyone who desired help. I decided to attend an afternoon session. Being still in uniform, I was conspicuous and, as I went up the stairs, the pastor met me and introduced himself. In a few words I tried to explain my need.

"What you need is the baptism of the Holy Spirit," was his prompt reply.

"Whatever I need, I need it badly," I answered. "I cannot go on as I have in the past."

It was three o'clock in the afternoon and the meeting was about to begin. He took me to their prayer room and introduced me to several people and left us. They were very kind and loving and, after listening to my problem and my desire to have some reality in my Christian experience, one replied, "We sense Christ's presence as we praise Him

The Reason Revealed

and thank Him for His love." And he suggested that I join with them in an act of worship.

I tried to do as they suggested, but their facility in prayer only made me more conscious than ever of my own need. Saying out loud, "Glory to God" and "Praise Jesus" was meaningless to my empty heart. At last they recognized this and let me pray as I felt led. They were kind, earnest people and prayed along with me. I was determined not to leave that room until I had experienced the "peace" which Jesus had promised to His disciples.

There was much which I had to review in my past. There were failures to confess and errors in judgment which needed to be recognized. As I prayed, self-will and pride began to loom larger and larger. I had to recognize them as the reason for my failure to witness to others. As I continued to wait before the Lord, I began to see that a failure to make a real commitment to Christ could be the cause of my lack of peace and joy which He had promised.

The afternoon meeting ended and more people joined the group. For me, time passed unnoticed and the evening service began. I had not found what I came for and the group encouraged me to continue seeking the Lord's blessing. I asked Him to help me and began to recognize His Hand in circumstances hitherto unnoticed. Then praise and thanksgiving began to come spontaneously.

It must have been after ten o'clock when suddenly the Lord lifted the burden and I felt His Presence and the joy and peace which He had promised. Awed by the experience but rejoicing, I must have arisen from my knees. Nothing in my Anglican background had prepared me for the "Hallelujahs" and "Glory to God" that filled the room, and I was rejoicing with them. I felt forgiven, cleansed, and had an inner peace and joy such as I had never experienced before.

Then someone insisted that I kneel again. I did not understand and they tried to explain that the evidence of God's full blessing was speaking "in tongues," that is, in an unknown language. I knelt again, but was confused and all I could do was thank the Lord for the blessings I had received and confess that I did not know what was missing.

I was dead in earnest and if there was more, I wanted it. As I prayed, I found that all I could do was to continue to thank God for the blessings received. I began to feel very tired and wanted to leave and so asked the Lord to give me what they felt was lacking. How gracious and loving is our God! Strange words came to my mind and were uttered almost involuntarily. The group lifted me to my feet and the room was filled again with praises to God. I was deeply grateful to these dear people for praying with me for so long and for the great help they had been, but I was confused and longed for quiet to think through and understand my experience. I had come into that room at three in the afternoon. It was almost eleven o'clock at night when I left.

The next day, still somewhat confused by all that had happened, I went to see a mature Christian friend and related my experience.

"If you had prayed eight minutes instead of eight hours and surrendered yourself to the Lord, the result would have been the same," was Sid's comment.

"You may be right," was my answer after a few moments of thought, "but I feel that time was needed for the Holy Spirit to bring to my mind the things that I had to confess. And time was needed for me to see the hindrances to a real and complete commitment to Christ. Without the encouragement and support of those dear people, I might not have persevered until I received the blessings I sought."

"God is never in a hurry," Sid replied, "and in your case, no doubt time was needed. The way to increased blessing is an ever fuller commitment to Christ, and this is not a one-time experience but a daily act of faith."

"I know you are right! This is the first time I have ever felt the presence of Christ as a living reality. I can feel His love and concern. I see what you mean--the more Christ has of us, the more we have of Him."

"Yes, and remember His promise. 'I will never leave thee nor forsake thee.'" (Heb. 13:5)

As we talked, Sid explained to me about the Pentecostal Movement. Some of my questions were cleared up. After prayer I left, thanking God for a Christian friend who would explain to a new believer what should be done to grow spiritually. I was beginning to see the truth of the promise, "Then shall you know, if you follow on to know the Lord." And there was born a feeling of expectancy. With all my heart I wanted to "follow on." How and where would God lead? With this thought came the conviction that a God-centered life could be one of adventure.

The armistice had been signed and the war was over. I waited impatiently for my discharge to come through. Some months passed and we were well into 1919 before I received it. Some months earlier, I had asked friends to pray that I might know God's will for my life, claiming the promise, "I will instruct you and teach you the way you should go; I will counsel you with my eye upon you." (Psalm 32:8 RSV) I recognized that God had saved my life in the war and that I had promised to do His will. Now the question was: How does God guide? I consulted my friends and read all I

The Reason Revealed

could find on the subject. The manner of God's guidance seemed as varied as the individuals involved, but all were in agreement that He does guide. In my dilemma I fell back on the promise given earlier, "Then shall we know, if we follow on to know the Lord." Another promise strengthened this conviction, "Thine ears shall hear a word behind thee, saying, This is the way, walk ye in it, when ye turn to the right hand, and when ye turn to the left." (Isaiah 30:21) This promise gave the assurance that if one were to mistake the way, God would intervene.

My sister, Muriel, suggested that it might be wise to take some training at Moody Bible Institute in Chicago. It would give time for the Lord to indicate whether he was calling me into full-time Christian service. Their catalogue was sent for and in going over it I saw all students were given three practical work assignments.

"I hope that when I get to Moody they do not assign me to distribute tracts or to preach in the open air," I said jokingly to Muriel.

"Why would you not want to do that kind of practical work?" she inquired.

"Oh, I would be embarrassed to preach on a street corner," I answered, "and as for giving out tracts, forget it!"

"We don't choose how we will serve the Lord," she replied. "He does the choosing."

How right she was, because when I learned of my practical work assignments the first week I was at Moody, two of them were the ones I had hoped to avoid. Accepting them as from the Lord, I found real joy and satisfaction in carrying them out.

Soon after starting my course at Moody I met the one who was to be my companion in forty-five years of Christian service. Geraldine Ely's parents had been missionaries in India and she had been named after Geraldine Taylor (Mrs. Howard Taylor), daughter-in-law of the founder of the China Inland Mission. When we became engaged, she wrote to her parents telling them that she had decided to take the rest of the name--Taylor.

Geraldine's special talent was the piano and at one time she had hoped to be a concert pianist. Very early in her teens, Geraldine began to play the piano at her father's meetings. Later she was on the faculty of the Curtis School of Music when it first began in Philadelphia. Then she felt God's call and came to Moody. I saw her as she played the piano at the first student assembly I attended, and immediately tried to meet her.

We both were interested in mission work around the world and frequently attended meetings of the Student Volunteer Movement. After some months, I desired to volunteer and then discovered that Geraldine was afraid that a mission board might not accept her because she was not strong physically. I did not want to press the issue and as the months passed, a certain complacency developed. We continued to vacillate until the beginning of our last term. Then a letter from Dr. E. J. Pace, Director of the Missionary Department, made me face the problem. He wrote:

I am strongly impressed to pen to you my feeling since Rev. Bingham's address this morning. In light of our conversation some time ago you appear to be marking time, uncertain of the Lord's leading...while Mr. Bingham was speaking you were singled out by the Spirit from all the students before me. So great was the pressure of prayer for you definitely, that I missed quite a chunk of his address. Frankly, it would distress me to see the Lord's program for you thwarted, which plan I am confident is out yonder where Christ has not been named. ...I do hope that you will not let the flame burn low; nor suffer obstacles to dissuade you from pressing onward....I would be glad to talk and pray over the matter with you, for my interest is keenly aroused.

With warm personal esteem, Your friend,

E. J. Pace.

An hour spent with Dr. Pace convinced me that I must pray more earnestly and systematically for clear guidance. He suggested that I consider Latin America as a possible field. Afterward, as I reviewed our conversation, it came to me that this had been God's way of saying, "This is the way, walk ye in it," for in a sense I had been turning away from Him by my complacency.

Therefore, I determined that at least the matter of volunteering for foreign mission work had to be settled. Instead of going to the Student Volunteer meeting that day, I decided to stay in my room and pray the matter through. Claiming the promise, "I will instruct thee and teach thee in the way which thou shalt go..." (Psalm 32:8). It was not long before I had the inward conviction that God wanted me to volunteer, that the foreign mission field was my place of service.

Having made that decision, it suddenly came to me that Geraldine did not feel led that way. In that case, our engagement was a mistake. If so, why had God brought us together? After a real struggle, I told the Lord that if she did not feel called to serve there, our engagement would have to be broken. To come to that decision was difficult,

The Reason Revealed

but having reached it, I had such peace of heart and mind that I was sure God had guided.

How very loving and gracious is our Heavenly Father!

My time of prayer was interrupted by a knock at the door. The president of the Student Volunteers was there. Having missed me at the meeting, he had come to find the reason for my absence. He also brought me startling news.

"You should have been at the meeting this afternoon. Miss Ely volunteered."

"She volunteered!" I exclaimed almost incredulously.

"Yes. She said that since coming into the meeting, God had convinced her that this was God's will for her!"

When I told him the reason for my absence, we had a time of rejoicing in God's goodness in guiding so clearly. I was to see Geraldine that evening and could hardly wait for the appointed hour. A rather contrite young lady met me in the lobby of the Women's Building.

"Norman, I did the most impulsive thing this afternoon," she exclaimed as we met. "I volunteered for the mission field without consulting you. I am so sorry..."

"You were not impulsive," I answered, interrupting her, "the Spirit of God moved you to do that in answer to my prayers."

"I don't understand!" she exclaimed.

"Of course you don't! I haven't told you why I was not at the meeting this afternoon. I spent the time in my room praying that God would guide us about volunteering. I decided that it was God's will for me and then prayed about our engagement. God in His goodness moved you to volunteer in the meeting. I am so glad we each did it independently. By His working it out in this wonderful way, it seems He is putting His hand on our hands and is saying, 'You are to serve me together in Latin America.'"

The evening was spent in rejoicing in God's goodness in revealing so clearly His plan for our lives. A few months later we graduated from Moody and were married in August, 1921.

We were still uncertain about our field of service, but this did not concern us because I felt definitely lead to continue my studies at a theological seminary. We had committed our future to the Lord and were resting in the promise, "I will instruct you and teach you in the way that you should go..." (Psalm 32:8) So confident were we that further guidance would be given that I jotted in the margin of my Bible "proven true" beside still another promise, "Thou will keep him in perfect peace, whose mind is stayed on Thee, because he trusteth in Thee." (Isaiah 26:3)

He continued to give His peace during my time in Xenia Seminary and when guidance was needed, He gave it. We were feeling definitely led toward service in Latin America. In my senior year in seminary, we applied to the Board of Foreign Missions of our Presbyterian denomination, were accepted and appointed to Mexico. We went there in September of 1923 and were assigned by the Mission to the city of Oaxaca in southern Mexico for language study.

We rejoiced in the clear guidance God had given and were convinced that He had led us to this place of service. Before many weeks had passed this conviction was to be rudely tested, but in the testings He was to prove again that His promises cannot fail.

4

PROMISED PROTECTION PROVIDED

When in physical danger during the First World War, I had become interested in the remarkable promises God has given us in His Word. Seeing many fulfilled in detail convinced me that in them God had given us a means by which He can become living and real in everyday life. The use of the personal pronoun in so many of the promises intrigued me and made it impossible to think of God as a far-off, impersonal influence. He is near, living, and real.

Two and one half months after arriving in Oaxaca a revolution broke out. By this time revolutions had ceased to have any pretense of social reforms, but were simply political. The governor of Oaxaca, a general, with some of his friends, started a revolution against the central or federal authorities. Most revolutions had been successful, but recently the United States had placed an embargo on the shipment of arms to Mexico. This revolution and a subsequent one failed. Since then there have been no further attempts.

During the time the revolutionary forces held the southern part of Mexico, from December 5, 1923, to April 1, 1924, we were completely cut off from the outside world. Now I had a wife and baby daughter to think about and it meant leaning harder upon God.

Also cut off with us were two couples, members of our mission. The Wolfes lived in a village on the railway, a short distance from the city. The Van Slykes were doing pioneer work among the mountain Indians, three or four days away by horse. While travel was still possible, we got together to plan how to meet the emergency. It was decided that all communications between us should be in English but, when possible, American slang would be used. With conditions so unsettled there was no telling into whose hands letters might fall. Since I was located in the city, it became my responsibility to keep the others supplied with funds and food extras. There was no problem in obtaining funds, because the merchants were afraid that the revolutionary government might levy special taxes and, to dispose of cash on hand, readily accepted drafts on our Mission Board in New York.

The situation became more critical when it was learned that the Serranos (the mountain Indians) had remained loyal to the central government and were surrounding the city. Their campfires on the mountainsides could be clearly seen at night.

One night, quite late, we were awakened by a pounding on our front door. Through the peephole in the big wooden door we saw that the intruders were revolutionary soldiers. When the pounding continued and became louder, we decided to respond.

"What do you want at this time of night?" we asked.

"We have come to take Sr. Taylor to headquarters," they responded.

"What do they want him for?"

"We don't know. We only have orders to bring him to headquarters."

"I am Sr. Taylor," I replied. "I will come to headquarters in the morning."

"Our orders are to bring you now. If you refuse to come, we will break down the door," was their gruff reply.

"Give me time to dress," I called back, "and I will go with you."

Half scared to death, not knowing why I was being arrested, I was marched through the silent streets, a soldier on either side and two or three behind. All sorts of fears came to mind but, at last, I was able to regain my composure and asked the Lord to fulfill His promise, "When they bring you before magistrates or powers, take no thought what things you shall answer...for the Holy Spirit shall teach you in that hour what you ought to say." (Luke 12:11 & 12) When we reached their headquarters, I was marched before a general. He looked me over, scowled, and said gruffly, "A spy has been arrested trying to slip into the city and he carried a letter addressed to you." From this and other things the general said, it became clear that I was being accused of communicating with the enemy.

"From whom is the letter, sir?" I inquired. "May I see it?"

The letter was passed to me and to my great relief I saw that it was from Arthur Wolfe. He needed some supplies and cash. Fortunately when asking for the letter, he had reverted to American slang and had written, "Shoot along some spondulix to the tune of a thousand." I then learned that they had tried to translate the letter with the help of a Spanish-English dictionary. "Dear Taylor," came out "Dear Tailor." And they had sent out to arrest a tailor who was under suspicion. Fortunately someone warned that man and he could not be found. Then they realized that Taylor was a surname and sent for me. In one part of the letter Wolfe used plain English,

"If Juan Cervantes comes in for his pay, do not give him anything. He has gone off with the Federal Forces." Juan had been a colporteur.

"General, may I ask you to have this paragraph translated? You will see that my friend is instructing me not to pay a certain man because he has gone off with the Federal Forces. Surely that proves that he is not supporting them."

Several heads bent over the dictionary and finally they told the general that I was right.

"Since your aides agree with me on what the paragraph says, may I ask that the man who brought this message be released. Clearly he is not a spy."

I think the general was beginning to feel just a little foolish about the whole matter, because he expressed his regrets that he had brought me to headquarters in the middle of night. Then to justify himself, he added, "It is well that you came now because if you had not, the young man would have been shot at dawn as a spy."

As I walked through the silent streets on my way home, the sound of my footsteps seemed almost joyous in contrast to the tramp, tramp, tramp of the soldiers' steel-studded boots as we had marched along this same street an hour before.

Arriving at home, I found that Geraldine had spent the time in prayer for my safety and together we knelt to thank the Lord for His presence and guidance. We were especially thankful that the young man's life had been spared and that I had not been asked to translate the request for funds. Next day we learned that the messenger was a seminary student who had come to Oaxaca for the Christmas holidays and had been cut off by the revolution.

In a letter which was written in installments to be mailed when the revolution ended, I find this sentence: "We live in peace of mind remembering that 'The Angel of the Lord encampeth around about them that fear Him, and delivereth them.'" (Psalm 34:7) He did keep us restful, trusting in Him.

Then one morning we were awakened by the sound of gunfire in the park on which our house faced. Immediately we knew that the Serranos had attacked. The patio was about three feet lower than the floor level of the house, so we put a mattress there and felt somewhat protected from stray bullets. Volley followed volley. It seemed almost endless. Bullets came through the shutters and one pierced the water tank on the roof. We watched the water flow out of the jagged holes.

While the fighting was in progress, we tried to keep our little Nan happy with her dolls and toys in our protected spot. For our own encouragement Geraldine and I took turns reading aloud familiar passages from the Bible. With the sound of gunfire in our ears, it was amazing how relevant and comforting were the words of the Psalmist written almost 3000 years ago.

"He that dwelleth in the secret place of the Most High shall abide under the shadow of the Almighty." (Psalm 91:1). As I read that verse it suddenly came to me that the overhanging verandah roof protected us from the hot tropical sun and I exclaimed to Geraldine, "Look, dear, at how the shadow of the roof symbolizes for us the Lord's protecting power."

"The same figure is used in Psalm 121," remarked Geraldine. "Let's look at that for a moment," and she read aloud, "The Lord is thy shade upon thy right hand. The sun shall not smite thee by day...The Lord shall preserve thee from all evil...' What a wonderful promise!"

We continued to read from the 91st Psalm, "Thou shalt not be afraid of the terror by night nor for the arrow that flieth by day....A thousand shall fall at thy side...but it shall not come nigh thee." Later we learned that our next door neighbor had been killed by the attackers but no one knocked on or even tried our doors.

I finished reading the 91st Psalm and continued in the 92nd. As we reached the 93rd Psalm, the fourth verse, a familiar army term came to mind and I reread it, "The Lord on high is mightier than the noise of battle; yea, than many waves of men."

"All this is confirmed by the Lord's own words," Geraldine suggested, as I closed my Bible. "Peace I leave with you, my peace I give unto you...Let not your heart be troubled, neither let it be afraid." (John 14:27). As we meditated, the thought came that this promise could also be considered a command.

Promised Protection Provided 33

This rather startled us! Together we bowed our heads and thanked God for His promises and His protection. A quiet peace and confidence filled our hearts and minds even as the sounds of fighting continued.

After several hours of heavy fighting in the park, the conflict seemed to move to the side streets leading to the center of the city. Evidently the revolutionary forces were retreating. The noise of gunfire slowly died away around noon and there was silence. About three o'clock in the afternoon the fighting suddenly erupted again and soon moved along the side streets into the park. There the attackers made a stand, but not for long, and the fighting slowly died away in the distance. The revolutionary forces had received reinforcements from a nearby town and had repulsed the attack. However, the Serrano campfires still could be seen at night and further attacks were threatened.

The very next day soldiers were again at our door. This time it was to advise us that they were taking our flat roof to make a machine gun emplacement. Soon the roof was encircled with sandbags. Realizing that if there should be another attack, our house would become a focal point for the fighting, we accepted an invitation from a neighbor and slept in their home. A squad of soldiers would come each evening and climb to the roof by a ladder in the patio. Then I would lock up the house, turn loose our Great Dane dog and go to the neighbor's. In the morning, I would return and find the soldiers clustered around the top of the ladder and Sultan sitting at its foot. Even though he was wagging his tail, they never came down before I arrived and tied him up.

The campfires continued to be seen on the mountainsides but nothing further happened until the beginning of April. My serial letter reads, "Yesterday morning we awoke to the splendid news that the revolutionary forces have evacuated the city. On verifying this, we immediately removed the sandbags from our roof and heaved a sigh of relief to be rid of them. Today the Federal Forces arrived in town with banners flying. Tonight we probably have 4,000 troops in town. April 13: Today it is stated that the first train with mail will arrive. Tomorrow our mail will go out. At last, after four months, we will have communication with the outside world."

For the first time in almost two months we slept at home! Our hearts were full of thanksgiving and praise to God for His overshadowing presence during the whole experience. This was our introduction to Mexico and we wondered whether even a long term of service could ever give us clearer evidence of God's faithfulness and loving-kindness. He had fulfilled in detail every promise we had claimed.

A few years later the Mexican government put into effect certain sections of their constitution which nationalized all church properties. At the same time, all priests and Protestant ministers not Mexican by birth were disqualified. All foreign priests were expelled from the country, but the Protestant missionaries, although we could not officiate as ministers, were allowed to reregister as professors. From the point of view of the authorities preaching was not the exclusive right of a priest, and so we were allowed to continue preaching, but could not administer the sacraments or direct a service. As is understandable, Catholic feelings ran very high and there was a marked increase in fanaticism and persecution of Protestants.

The Van Slykes, who were working among the Zapateco Indians, were away on furlough, and I was asked to make periodic visits to their village. Very early on the morning of May 27, 1926, I started on a trip to Yatzachi el Bajo, where they served. It was 3 a.m., but before I left Geralding and I read the Daily Light for that day and, in prayer, claimed promises for the trip. "The Lord is good, a stronghold in the day of trouble; and He knoweth them that trust in Him," (Nahum 1:7) was claimed especially.

The dry season was almost over but the rains had not begun. As a result, the trails were carpeted with a thick layer of dust, making travel very unpleasant. At noon the next day we reached a spot where the narrow trail widened, leaving an open space to the windward. It seemed a good spot to eat our lunch free from dust. We had just tied up our horses when in the distance we saw a great cloud of dust rising from the trail. It was a pack train of forty to fifty heavily laden mules. Above the cloud of dust there seemed to float four large sombreros below which there finally emerged the muleteers. The dust was so thick that their noses and mouths were covered with bandanas, giving them a bandit-like appearance. With loud shouts and curses they urged on the mules and we guessed at once that they had been drinking heavily.

As they reached my companion, they stopped to ask who I was. Two of them approached me and their antagonism could be felt. To my consternation, the first man swaggered up and announced, "You're the man we were told to kill." I could hardly believe my ears!

"Wait a minute," said his companion who was right behind. "I have never talked to a *'Protestante.'* I want to ask him some questions. We can always kill him later. We have our guns, too."

Promised Protection Provided

His reference to guns puzzled me. I never carried one. Then I realized that they had mistaken my camera case, which was on my belt, for a gun holster.

"Why don't you worship the Virgin Mary?" the second man asked.

"We honor her above all the women who have ever lived. She was used by God to bring the Savior Jesus Christ into the world. She has our love and respect."

"Do you worship God or the devil?" he then demanded gruffly.

"God is the only one to worship. Through faith in Jesus Christ He becomes our heavenly Father and wants to bless us."

Other questions followed and the atmosphere seemed less tense.

"I am a friend of all Mexicans," I volunteered, "and I am here for the single purpose of trying to help everyone find the greater blessings which God has for all."

"If you are a friend of Mexicans, drink with us," came the harsh retort, and before I knew it he had thrust a bottle into my hand.

"Thank you very much, but I do not drink *aguardiente*," (a distilled liquor) and placing the bottle on the ground, I stepped back several paces, picked up a heavy stick and placed my hand on my camera case. My helper, sensing the danger, rushed to my side.

The muleteers whipped out their knives and took several steps toward us. Evidently they had been bluffing about having guns. At that very moment, when they were preparing to attack, one of the other men shouted that the mules were leaving the trail and might lose their packs. Waving their knives and cursing us, they went down the road to regroup their pack train. We watched them disappear in the distance and then, still shaken by our experience, sat down on the ground to eat our lunch. Before doing so, we bowed our heads and thanked God that He is a "stronghold in the day of trouble." There was no similarity between my camera case and a gun holster; God had caused them to make the mistake.

Late that afternoon we reached a silver mine called "La Natividad." The miners were all Mexican, but the superintendent and his wife were Americans and had invited me to stop with them any time I came their way. He was a Protestant and she a Catholic. They were always very hospitable and I appreciated their friendship.

"Will you please say grace," my host requested as we sat down at the dinner table. As the meal was served, he inquired, "How are things in Oaxaca and what news is there of our mutual friends?"

"There is considerable unrest because of the enforcement of the new religious laws, but that is to be expected," and then I turned the conversation to what had happened among their friends.

"Have you personally had any trouble?" my host inquired. After some hesitation I decided to tell them of my experience that noon.

"Yes," I replied. "This noon I was threatened by some drivers of a mule train but for two reasons they did not attack. Fortunately, they mistook the camera case on my belt for the holster of a gun. Also, at the very moment when they might have attacked, the mules began to stray off the trail and there was danger of their packs slipping off." After I had related details of what had happened, there was a long silence.

"It may surprise you to learn," said my host at last, "that we had a letter from Oaxaca asking us not to receive you as you came by on this trip."

I was surprised, and waited rather anxiously for him to go on.

"I answered that it had always been our custom to welcome into our home friends of both faiths and that I knew of no reason to change. Furthermore, I allow no one to dictate to me whom we may have in our home! Continue to stop with us any time you pass this way." And his wife added her cordial invitation.

That night, reviewing the events of the day, I thanked God for the certainty of His promises and also for faithful Christian friends. The Lord had proven again, in an unmistakable way, that His Promises cannot fail!

A few weeks after this experience I was in Mexico City and, at a service in Union Church, met an old southern gentleman who had come to Mexico to see the missionary work done by his denomination. We began to chat, and I was impressed by his joyous spirit.

"As a boy did you ever have a lucky coin?" he asked suddenly.

"What boy hasn't?" was my prompt reply.

"I have the best lucky coin that anyone ever possessed. It has helped me in making decisions; has helped me in my business; and indeed in every phase of my life." He had a twinkle in his eyes and I responded in exactly the way he knew I would.

"If you have such a coin, I would like to see it."

"I will not only show it to you but I will give you one," he said with a broad, contagious smile. Reaching into his pocket, he produced a coin about the size of a fifty cent piece. On one side was the single word, "Pray," and below it

Promised Protection Provided

the Bible promise, Jeremiah 33:3, "Call upon me, and I will answer thee, and show thee great and mighty things, which thou knowest not." On the reverse side there was the reminder: "Don't forget to pray" with another Bible promise.

"Then you believe in claiming Bible promises!" I exclaimed.

"Indeed I do! My life and my business have been built on them in recent years."

I knew that I had found a kindred spirit in Mr. J. C. Allerdyce of San Antonio, Texas, and listened with keen interest as he told how God had worked in his life. Of special interest were his stories of how he used his lucky coin come-on in seeking to win other men to Christ. He had been a candy manufacturer and had retired.

"I am here," he continued, "to see our mission work and to help in any way I can in the churches." I had already learned that he knew very little Spanish and doubts began to come to mind that his help could be very effective. But I soon found that I had underestimated Mr. Allerdyce. His lucky coin showed that he had original ideas and I was sure that when using it, he rarely failed to open a conversation on spiritual matters. But how could he help in the churches? His plan for helping was just as original as his lucky coin.

"One of the difficulties in your work, I know, is the false idea that people have about Protestants. All sorts of absurd stories are believed, and new people are afraid to come into our churches or halls. If the curiosity of the people can be sufficiently aroused, they will come in spite of their superstitions. I don't know Spanish, but I do know how to make candy. A sweet tooth is universal. I have given candy-pulls in several churches in the Federal District and new people have attended. Could you use me in Oaxaca?"

"Could we use you? I know that we could! I don't know how to say candy-pull in Spanish, but come when you can. A candy-pull could bring real joy into the peoples' drab lives and help to lift their burdens for a while. They have few amusements; this would be a bright spot and make them happy...and through it some new people may be open to our message."

Several weeks later Mr. Allerdyce arrived and we had plans that surprised even him. After a candy-pull in the city church and in a nearby town, I suggested that we go out to the mountain village of Yatzachi el Bajo. The Van Slykes were still on furlough and it was time for another visit, especially since word had come that attendance at services had dwindled to a handful. Perhaps we could arouse the curiosity of the villagers and by attending a candy-pull they would learn that Protestants did not have "horns and tails," as some believed.

"It will be a four-day ride, Mr. Allerdyce. Do you think you can stand that?" I asked anxiously. I remembered that he was over seventy years old.

"I have kept in good shape playing golf. I am sure that I can take it."

"I am sorry to have to tell you," I answered laughingly, "on a four-day ride you will discover that you have muscles you never knew you possessed." But he was game!

With two pack horses, one loaded with five-gallon cans of glucose, we were soon on our way. We cut the daily distance slightly and tried to stop every couple of hours to rest. Although he must have had many sore muscles, Mr. Allerdyce never complained and was always contagiously happy. Even the men with us, although they could not understand what he said, caught his joyous spirit.

The fourth day we reached the village and told the few believers to spread the news about the candy-pull. I have no idea how much the villagers believed, but, when one morning two of our men set off with a pack horse for a nearby village where the weekly market was held, they knew something unusual was going to happen. They were convinced when the men returned with the horse laden with over a hundred pounds of big cakes of brown sugar.

Even in the market our men created a sensation. To get the amount of sugar required, they had to go from one merchant to another. No one wanted to sell so much sugar, fearing that he would not have enough for his regular customers. Everyone wanted to know why so much was needed. So the news of the candy-pull spread everywhere. Curiosity was aroused by the unanswerable question: What is a candy-pull?

Suddenly we were confronted with a problem. At first glance it seemed insurmountable! At breakfast the third day Mr. Allerdyce asked a simple question and I was left aghast at my stupidity.

"Norm, where do you keep the pots which we are to use to make all this candy?"

"Oh what a blunder!" I confessed after a few moments' silent consternation. "I never thought of utensils. Everyone here cooks in little clay pots which hold only a quart or two."

"It would take fifty pots of that size to cook all the taffy for the crowd you are expecting. Better find out at once if there are any larger utensils of any kind in the

Promised Protection Provided

village," said Mr. Allerdyce. For once, there was no twinkle in his eye.

Feeling extremely foolish for not having thought of the need for several large pots, I went out to consult with the members of the congregation.

"Fidencio, do any of the believers have really big pots?" I asked the leader of the congregation. Not having any word for pot in Spanish, I used the one which meant clay utensil.

"No, *señor*!" he answered immediately. " A really big one would have to be made to order."

"Why do you ask, Sr. Taylor?" inquired his wife, Mercedes.

"We have to have some big pots to make all that taffy. I never thought of the matter, or we could have brought some big metal ones from the city. I don't know what we can do!" I replied, almost in exasperation.

"O, *señor*, don't you worry," Mercedes replied. "That is no problem."

"What do you mean? Who has some?" I asked in surprise.

"Every woman in the village has a five gallon can which she uses to bring water from the well. Look, there is mine. How many will you need?"

Bless her dear heart, she had the solution to our problem. Then for good measure she added a bit of worldly wisdom which would never have occurred to me.

"*Señor*, we will promise to return the cans unwashed and so for several days they can all do their cooking with sweet water."

"Mercedes, I will leave it all up to you. I will ask Mr. Allerdyce how many cans he will need and you can promise the women that we will leave a little taffy in each one."

"I have found someone who has the wisdom of Solomon, and our problem is solved," I told Mr. Allerdyce. "But she happens to be a lady." And we had a great laugh as I gave him the details.

"She is well named," he added. "She has done us a favor and also a favor to those who will loan us their pots."

The eventful day came finally, and early in the afternoon Mr. Allerdyce began to make his preparations. He was master of ceremonies and he kept us all busy.

"Norm, have the boys put rocks for the kettles to stand on. See that the stones are level. Then get them to build fires, big ones, over each set of rocks, and when they burn down we will put the cans of taffy on the coals. Also, we will need several hundred squares of paper on which to serve the taffy. The boys could get them cut up. And we will need all the tables you can find..."

It was a busy afternoon in the back yard! The sugar and the glucose had been measured out and the right quantity in each pot. Soon there was a row of glowing coals to receive them. In the growing dusk, as Mr. Allerdyce went from pot to pot mixing the taffy, he found it warm work and, to the big apron he was wearing, he added a handkerchief around his forehead.

"In your get-up you remind me of a well-known biblical character," I called to him.

"Who is that?"

"The witch of Endor!"

"But hers was a vile brew, while mine is a sweet one," he replied.

The sun had touched the western mountains and it was time for us to call the villagers to the fiesta and soon the long blasts of a cow horn were echoing across the valley. White clad figures began appearing on the mountain trails, all converging on the mission house.

"Fidencio, when the people begin to arrive, have Poncho start playing music on the gramophone. When you think most of the people are here, let me know and you interpret my word of welcome. Then have Vicente read the Scripture in Zapateco and you give your message. And, by the way, when you finish your message, explain to the people what we mean by a candy-pull. I will have to be in the back yard to interpret for Sr. Allerdyce."

"Yes, *señor*. Don't worry, we will care for things here."

The people began to arrive in groups and soon all the chairs were occupied and they had to sit on the ground. As there was an opportunity, I slipped away from the backyard activities and shook hands with as many as possible. They continued to crowd in and soon the verandah was full and they began to sit in the patio.

"*Señor, señor!*" said Fidencio excitedly. "There are almost a hundred people here! Shall we begin?" My word of welcome was soon given and I was back in the yard where I was needed because most of the candy was about done and the pots had to be taken from the fires to cool. When I thought Fidencio's message would be about over, I slipped away to the front and found he was explaining what to do when they received the taffy. As he was speaking in their language, I did not know what he was saying, but when I saw him press his thumbs against the first two fingers of his hands and move his hands slowly apart, I knew that a demonstration was needed to show how to pull taffy.

"Fidencio, please tell the people that the boys will put a dab of lard on their hands and they are to spread it all over their hands to keep the candy from sticking. Then I will demonstrate how to pull the taffy."

At that moment the boys appeared and put about a teaspoonful of lard on each pair of outstretched hands. Obediently they rubbed their hands together but then I noticed that some could not resist licking the lard off...with amusing results later.

In the back yard, Mr. Allerdyce was pouring out the taffy on the squares of paper we had spread on the tables. When the first batch he had poured was cool enough to handle, I took what was on two sheets and started for the front yard, calling one of the small boys to follow me.

"Juan, follow right behind me and keep saying, 'When you get your taffy, do what Sr. Taylor is doing.'"

At first I was only able to pull the taffy out a foot or so, but as it hardened it was possible to pull my hands much further apart and still catch the center before it could fall. The Indians were greatly amused.

Then the boys appeared with trays piled high with heaps of candy on the sheets of paper. Never have I seen Indians laugh as those did! The ones who had licked the lard off or had not spread it properly now found their hands sticking together. Those who had followed the instructions saw that their candy was turning whiter, as were their hands also!

As I marched back and forth, I saw a little five-year-old whose hands were stuck together and he was bawling to the full capacity of his lungs. However, above the laughter of the others he could hardly be heard. As my taffy was about ready to eat, I stopped by the little boy, broke off a generous lump and popped it into his open mouth. Immediately the crying stopped and slowly a broad grin spread across his little tear-stained face.

After the people had pulled their taffy, other squares of paper were offered to those who wanted to take some home. Everybody was in a very happy mood and more music was requested. Other records were played for perhaps an hour. Finally we said, *"Buenas noches"* (good night) to all and thanked them for coming.

Two boys were placed at the entrance to the patio holding large pitch-pine torches from which the people could light their own as they left. Standing at the gate to say good night to the people, Mr. Allerdyce and I watched as they climbed the mountain trails to their homes. In the darkness they looked like dozens of fireflies scattered across the mountainside. One by one, the lights disappeared and we stood alone in the darkness. Mr. Allerdyce seemed to have forgotten my presence, for I heard him pray, "Dear Lord, I thank you! I thank you! We called and you have answered as you promised. May many of these people learn to know and love you. Thank you for giving me this experience. I would not have missed it for anything."

As we slowly and silently entered the house I thanked God for this dear man and for the inspiration he had been to all of us. He had been so ready to help others!

Some years before this experience with Mr. Allerdyce, God had gone to the other extreme and had brought a rich blessing through a very small child.

5

A CHILD'S SILENCE SPOKE VOLUMES

"I must spend the whole morning in language study," I said to my wife as we finished breakfast. "Please do not allow anyone to disturb me."

"I will see that you are undisturbed," Geraldine replied. "I realize that your next language exam is only a few weeks away and you must have time to study."

Our little four-year-old daughter was in her high chair and paused in her eating for a moment as we talked. As I passed by her, I ran my hand through her curly fair hair, and went to my office and soon was immersed in the study of irregular verbs. An hour or two must have passed when there came a knock at the door of my study.

"Who is there?" I called rather impatiently.

There was no reply, but the heavy wooden door slowly opened as a curly fairhead came around the corner.

"What do you want, Nan?"

"I don't want anything, Daddy," came her reply. "I just want to sit near you." And she came through the door carrying a little chair in her hand.

"I do not want to be disturbed," came to my lips but was suppressed before it could be spoken. "Let her come in," I said to myself. "She will begin to chatter in a few moments and then I can put her out of the room."

With her little chair in her hand, she came across the room and placed it near mine. She was perfectly quiet and I tried to return to my language study, but her words kept coming to mind. "I don't want anything, Daddy. I just want to sit near you."

Five minutes passed and still no word from her. When would the child speak? Another five minutes and then she got up, but just moved her chair a little nearer to mine.

Her words kept ringing in my ears, and suddenly the pages of grammar seemed to become blurred. "Why are you getting so emotional?" I demanded of myself and tried to blink my eyes clear but the letters still were unreadable. Another five minutes passed. "When would the child speak?" The longer she sat silently right beside me, the harder it was becoming to dismiss her from the room.

I wanted to get up and take the dear child in my arms but that would have spoiled the whole thing. She was recognizing my request to be undisturbed, not realizing that her presence and her continued silence were more devastating to my concentration than a half dozen visits from pastors or believers from the villages.

It must have been almost twenty-five minutes when she suddenly got up, picked up her chair and walked to the door. As she opened it, she turned and said, "Thank you, Daddy." And the heavy door closed behind her.

"Thank you, Daddy, for what?" I asked myself. "For letting me sit near you," would have been her answer. As I thought on the matter, suddenly a spiritual application came to mind and I bowed my head in prayer.

"O God, my heavenly Father, have I ever asked to come into your Presence just to be near you? Have I ever come to you without petitions and needs? Have I ever been satisfied just to worship? I have continually pressed my requests. You have said in your Word that 'A little child shall lead them.' One has today! Thank you for the lesson in silence and worship. Forgive my 'chattering' in my praying. Help me to learn the value of waiting quietly before you, that I may hear your voice."

As a result of this experience, I found that my daily devotions became more meaningful and my Bible reading much more helpful. A careful study of the fifteenth chapter of John gave me fresh insights into the secret of successful missionary work.

"You know how frustrated I have felt about my work," I said to Geraldine one day. "Today in my Bible reading the Lord showed me a vital truth: 'Without Me you can do nothing!' (John 15:5) We must recognize this fact and, when we do, then He makes this amazing promise: 'I have chosen you and ordained you, that you should go and bring forth fruit, and that your fruit shall remain.' (John 15:16). Thus the Lord shows clearly that in ourselves we can do nothing but promises His Presences and Power when we trust Him. Why does it take us so long to see these truths?"

A Child's Silence Spoke Volumes

In our daily devotions we continued to ask God to guide us how to expand our evangelistic outreach and enable us to touch more people. One day after our prayer together Geraldine exclaimed, "You have been distributing tracts in the market places, but had you thought of the possibility of sending literature to people by mail?"

"That's a good idea. But to whom? The people in the villages are the ones who accept tracts gladly because they have little reading material. The city people just throw the tracts away, so the telephone directory is useless as a source for names." But the possibility of using the mails intrigued us and we continued to pray about this possibility.

"Geraldine!" I called as I returned home one day. "I have good news for you. Today I met Don Luis and mentioned your suggestion about sending literature by mail. He tells me the government publishes a directory of public officials and suggested where I might get a copy."

"That would give us a list of hundreds of officials in small towns and villages to whom we could mail a Gospel portion and some tracts. When are you going to see if you can get a copy of this directory?"

"Right after lunch, because some of the government offices close early in the afternoon." This I did and was given a copy. When I offered to pay for it, I was told that there was no charge. Thrilled by seeing God work, I hurried home.

"I not only got the directory," I exclaimed to Geraldine as I met her in the hall, "but it is far more complete than I had expected. It not only gives the names and addresses of the village presidents and the municipal secretaries, but also lists all schoolteachers, railway agents, and postmasters. By addressing the literature to the official by his title rather than his name, we need not change our mailing lists when the officials change."

"How thankful I am that you were able to get this directory. It gives us an almost limitless supply of names."

"Yes, that is true. Now let's ask the Lord to give us a promise on which to base our distribution."

It was not long before both of us felt convinced that Isaiah 55:11 was the confirming promise we sought. "My Word...shall not return void; but it shall accomplish that which I please, and shall prosper in the thing whereto I sent it."

When checking on postal rates, I discovered that if instead of using envelopes we made up the literature in rolls, using the post office wrappers, we would save both time and money.

About this time I was led to see a truth in the Parable of the Sower (Matthew 13:3-8) that is so obvious that it seemed incredible that I had overlooked it in my study of this passage. God's Word is the seed. In four verses we read of the failures because of bad soil conditions, but the successful harvest is summed up in one verse of the narrative. I had been too conscious of the failures and it suddenly dawned on me that the major part of the seed fell upon good ground and brought an abundant harvest, "Some an hundredfold, some sixtyfold and some thirtyfold."

In distributing God's Word could we expect similar results? Why not? So we mailed hundreds of rolls of literature all over Mexico with the expectation of a bountiful harvest. We were not disappointed! The many letters received and the requests for more literature showed the hunger there was for God's Word. It simply amazed us!

To show the "good ground" upon which the seed fell, I would quote two letters. The first came from a little village in Guerrero. The municipal secretary had written us for more literature. Perhaps it was in response to his second or third request that we sent him a copy in Spanish of "The Way to God," by D. L. Moody. The Spirit of God had worked through the printed page, for he wrote us this amazing letter:

Dear Brethren:

I received the little book, the New Testament and also "The Way to God," by Moody, which books I have read. They have let me understand the truths therein. I give thanks to God our Saviour and Our Redeemer, Jesus Christ, that my brethren, The Seed Sowers, have remembered us in these forgotten mountains, disinherited of the knowledge of these truths. I thank God that through you the Light of the Truth has been sent into these gloomy mountains. We are more than delighted to know the Truth.

On Sunday the 7th we had a meeting of nearly one hundred peasants from different communities of this municipality. We had great success in the meeting. Tears were shed among those present, hearts were softened, and some cried out because of the darkness within them, only having known God through the images made by sculptors.

Our Lord Jesus Christ will save us by faith we have in Him. He will be merciful to us. No one here speaks Spanish, so I have been explaining the message of these books in their dialect, which is Tlapaneco. If you should care to send us more

books about God and Our Saviour Jesus Christ, I
shall continue to explain these truths. I sub-
scribe myself your brother and servant of God. I
send cordial greetings to you, who have been united
to us through Jesus Christ. He alone can unite us.

We showed this letter to a young missionary couple, Mr.
and Mrs. H. V. Lemley, who were seeking a field of work
among the Indians. God guided them to the Tlapaneco Indians
and today there are large portions of the New Testament in
two or three dialects. Also, there is a Bible school for
the training of Tlapaneco workers.

Through a friend, Dr. Kenneth Pike, who at that time was
working among the Mixteco Indians, we had another insight
into what happened when these rolls of literature were received. Until he recently retired, Dr. Pike was professor
of linguistics at the University of Michigan at Ann Arbor.
Also, he is a linguistic consultant for the Wycliffe Bible
Translators, with whom he was at the time his letter was
written:

For some years I have known a young fellow by
the name of Cavetano Sanchez. He is smooth faced,
well dressed for this ktown, ruddy, and had just finished the sixth grade of school....This year when I
came back and was thinking about a possible translation helper, he was the one who came to my mind
and I prayed about it. That, in spite of the fact
that I had never spoken to him about the Lord.

One day while working downstairs, he came in,
hat on, blanket over his arm, and a cheery smile,
as usual. After the usual greeting, I noticed that
he had a little blue Gospel in his hand.

"What's that?" I asked, wondering where he got
it.

"Oh, a little book."

"Let me see it. A Gospel of John! What does it
say?"

"Here is what it says," he explained, opening
the frontispiece.

There I saw "Los Sembradores." I did not know
who they were, but then remembered I had seen a reference to them in your article in Moody Monthly.
It seems that the mailman received them and gave
him one...

"What does it say?" I asked him about the
verses on the slip pasted on the frontispiece.
"Can you read them?"

"Of course I can read them," and he read the
first one.

"What does it say?" I asked.

"I don't know," he replied.

So we began to translate together and worked through all the verses. (Note--All the verses were on salvation and ended with an invitation to receive Christ.) I asked him if he wanted a pen to sign it.

"Shall I put my name here?" he asked.

"Yes, if you really believe what it says," I answered, "but don't if you do not." So he put his name on the line and then we went upstairs.

"Will you write it in Mixteco?" he asked.

"All right, if you help me." And we worked over the verses more slowly.

"I'll make a copy on the typewriter, and you can sign that, too." The copy was made.

"Shall I sign here?" he asked. This time he put his signature with all the curlicues they love to use.

His father is the "cantor" in the Catholic Church....One day I saw him sitting by the roadside reading a New Testament he had borrowed. Truly one sows and another reaps.

The literature we sent was all in Spanish and it is true, as in the case of Cayetano, many of the Indian young people who attend the government schools did not really understand Spanish. But it was amazing how, when their curiosity was aroused, they would find someone, as in this case, who could help them understand. In many cases, this meant reaching two people instead of one.

Truly God's Word is Life, and only He knows how many lives were transformed by the reading of these tracts and Gospel portions. They were distributed as "seed" to be watched over and watered by God, the Holy Spirit. Only the Master of the Harvest knows the results. Our part was to sow His Seed, and the many letters received indicated that much fell upon good ground. Therefore, we believe that God fulfilled His promises; that His Word did not return void, but prospered and accomplished what He had purposed.

His promises never fail! Very soon this fact was, again, to be proven true in my personal experience.

6

FAITH IS BETTER THAN SIGHT

"I am very sorry to have to tell you that the examinations and test indicate that you have amoebic dysentery, chronic malaria and there is the possibility that you have incipient sprue." The speaker was Dr. Garnett in Mexico City. I had come to the city for an executive committee meeting and, after being there a few days, had come down with a bad attack of chills and fever which had sent me to the doctor. I was feeling miserable!

"What do you recommend, doctor?" I asked. "I suppose it means hospitalization and continued treatments?"

"Yes, and the amoebic dysentery seems so established that it will be hard to eradicate," he replied.

His prognosis proved true. A three-week stay in the hospital with quinine every two hours night and day eliminated the malaria. But the other diseases remained unchanged and left little strength for daily duties.

A few months before, we had been transferred to Merida, Yucatan to reorganize a small training school into a Bible institute. Geraldine and I had found real joy in teaching the students and hoped that we might have years of service in that institution. However, the tropical climate accentuated the development of the sprue, which Dr. Garnett had seen as incipient, and I continued to lose weight. Then Geraldine contracted malaria, which seemed the last straw!

We were so thrilled and thankful at seeing the Bible Institute develop that we tried hard to stay on the field by laying hold of the promise, "Fear not, for I am with thee; be not dismayed, for I am thy God: I will strengthen thee, yea I will uphold thee with the right hand of my righteousness." (Isaiah 41:10). It strengthened our spirits but our physical condition remained unchanged. Our local doctor shattered any hope we have have had of remaining in that tropical climate.

"Taylor, the sooner you get out of this heat, the better for both you and Mrs. Taylor," he said after a periodic examination. "There is little hope for your recovering your health if you stay here." His report went to New York.

Then it was decided that we should return to the States on a health furlough, that I might be under the care of a tropical disease specialist in New York. Some months of treatment, including hospitalization, made him feel that both the amoebic dysentery and the sprue had been eradicated. To help re-establish my health, he thought a colder climate might serve as a stimulant and recommended that I return to my home in Winnipeg, Canada. However, forty-below-zero temperatures did not seem to help, but rather hindered my recovery.

To have months pass with no signs of improvement was very discouraging! In times of depression, which came frequently, another promise in Isaiah brought relief and even hope. "Strengthen ye the weak hands and confirm the feeble knees...be strong, fear not, behold, your God...will come and save you." (Isaiah 35:3 & 4). In weakness it was something to cling to and it worked!

At this time I read again the biography of David Livingstone and was encouraged by the entry in his journal when he faced a horde of hostile natives. He had written, "Jesus said, 'Lo I am with you always.' This is the word of a gentleman of most sacred and strictest honor. He will not break his promise." The opposition had disappeared by morning. I tried hard to believe the promise of Isaiah 35: that God would restore my health, but it was not easy!

As spring turned to summer, we rented a cottage at Pelican Lake, Minnesota and moved down there. A fourth child, a son, Norman, had been born in April. Four small children can make a lot of noise. Not wanting to curb their activities, but needing rest and quiet, I pitched a tent in the woods back of the cottage.

We had been at the lake only a few weeks when a letter came from the Mission Board. To me it was as devastating as an earthquake and I was forced to cast myself completely on the Lord. The gist of the letter was that the specialist had reported that I could never again serve in a tropical climate, that I now must live in a temperate one in order to maintain good health. Therefore, the conclusion was that it might be well to look for work at home since

Faith Is Better Than Sight 51

further work in the mission field seemed unlikely. It was
hard to believe what I was reading, for our hearts were in
our mission work.

"Geraldine, read this letter," I said to my wife, who
was sitting nearby going over the rest of the mail. "It
seems to close the door on our returning to Mexico!"

"It may be the doctors' opinion," she replied after she
had read the letter, "but that does not mean it is God's
will." She had more faith than I.

As I read and reread the letter, it seemed that the very
bottom had fallen out of my world. What should I do?
Where should I turn? My health was gone and I had a family
of five dependent on me. Doubts began to come about the
doctors' conclusions. Was I really cured of these tropical
diseases? Other doubts and fears filled my mind. In desperation I went out to the tent in the woods and, as I
knelt beside the cot, I spread the letter before the Lord.

With my Bible open at the book of Isaiah, which had
meant so much to me during my illness, my reading soon
turned into prayer as my eyes fell upon familiar passages.
I reminded the Lord of His promise: to be with us; to not
let us be dismayed; to strengthen, guide and save us from
our present situation. As I prayed, the Lord's presence
became very real.

After a while I began to read my Bible again, starting
where it was open at the forty-second chapter. As I read,
suddenly the sixteenth verse took on special meaning! I
reread it. The verse seemed to almost stand out from the
page. "I will bring the blind by a way that they knew not;
I will lead them in paths that they have not known; I will
make darkness light before them, and crooked things
straight. These things I will do unto them and not forsake
them." (Isaiah 42:16).

I reread the verse several times and my wonder grew as
the significance of the promise dawned on me. Could anyone
be blinder than I? But light was promised and new paths
too. How wonderful was the latter, since our old work
seemed closed in view of the specialist's recommendation.
Could this promise apply to me? The question had hardly
come to mind when my eyes fell on the nineteenth verse:
"Who is blind but my servant" I read aloud excitedly.

"O God, I thank you for your goodness," I prayed spontaneously. "Nothing could more fully meet my needs. I am
blind as to the future but seek to do your will. You promise light in the midst of darkness; new paths of service;
and above all, there is your promise not to forsake me. I
believe it and claim it. Fulfill your perfect will in us."

As I continued to pray and rejoice in God's faithfulness, a quiet peace and confidence filled my being, and with it came a spirit of expectancy. Where and how would God work? Suddenly I felt the urge to share all this with Geraldine.

"Geraldine, where are you?" I called as I hurried down the pathway toward the cottage. "God has given an answer to our problem. The Board's letter has closed the possibility of our returning to Yucatan but God has promised something far better."

"Look at this promise!" I exclaimed as I sat beside her on the lounge. Together we read and reread the verse and then together claimed it, rejoicing in its promise for the future.

From that day on, together we thanked God for the minuteness of the promises He had given. They really staggered our imagination! What more could one ask? Our prayers were filled with rejoicing and thanksgiving for His promise for the future. The whole atmosphere of our home changed radically. How could one feel depressed after having been given a promise like this by God? A moment of rejoicing in the Lord's faithfulness caused depression to dissipate as fog does before the rising sun.

Then a glimmer of light began to come in our darkness of uncertainty about the future. Newspapers from Mexico City brought word of construction work being done on the highways from the city to nearby towns. Roads to Puebla, Toluca and Cuernavaca were being widened and improved. The international highway was being constructed from both ends and was progressing rapidly. We followed the reports with great interest and with them came an idea.

"The specialist recommended that you should work in a temperate climate, dear," Geraldine said one day after our prayer time. "Has it occurred to you that there are a few climates more temperate than the 'perennial springtime' of Mexico City? I wonder whether there could be any work for us there?"

"Now that you bring up that matter," I replied, "ever since reading about the improvement in the highways around Mexico City the thought has been in my mind that a Gospel car might be a very effective way to evangelize the region. Let's make it a matter for daily prayer. Perhaps this may be the unknown paths that the promise mentions."

Meanwhile my health began to improve rapidly. Indeed the improvement came so quickly after having cast myself upon the Lord, claiming Isaiah 42:16, that we could attribute it only to Him. A visit to the Mayo Clinic in Rochester, Minnesota brought a most encouraging report. They

Faith Is Better Than Sight

felt that I could safely work in the climate of Mexico City and that within a few months I should be able to return to the field. Immediately I wrote to the Board and the Mission suggesting the Gospel car project and offering to donate my own car. The matter was given favorable consideration and it was agreed that we could return to Mexico the following February.

As we prayed over the project and made detailed plans, the whole matter was confirmed in a remarkable way. The car was to be equipped with a radio, which was still a novelty in those days, as well as with a phonograph, slide projector and so forth. A church had invited me to speak at its midweek prayer meeting and I told them about the Gospel car project. The pastor and the people all seemed very interested.

"What will the radio cost?" the pastor inquired.

"Seventy-five dollars delivered in Mexico City," was my prompt reply.

"All of us are interested in your project and would like to give the radio," he said. "We will take up an offering now and what is lacking can be made up from our mission fund."

While the ushers took up the offering and counted it, we sang several hymns. One of the ushers laid a paper on the pulpit and as the pastor read the note, his face registered surprise.

"Brethren, I think God is in this project," and then after a pause he counted, "The offering just taken amounts to seventy-four dollars and sixty cents."

Spontaneously the congregation broke into applause. Geraldine and I could hardly believe our ears. To have the offering amount to practically the sum needed seemed a confirmation of God's leading and filled us with delight.

Meanwhile we had been in correspondence with the Mission. It was found that someone was needed to teach two subjects in the theological seminary. It was suggested that I might do this as well as head up the Gospel car project. The gift of our car was accepted, but they suggested that it be sold when we returned to the field and the proceeds donated towards the purchase of a car in Mexico.

As soon as the family was established in Mexico City, I began to teach in the seminary. Also talks began with the Mission treasurer about the funds for the purchase of the Gospel car. The 'Great Depression' was beginning, and six months had brought drastic changes in finances. The Mission budget had been cut, the schools had deficits and there were no extra funds available. Weeks passed and the case seemed hopeless.

To make matters worse, the church which had given the radio began to write for news of the project. Finally some money was found for running expenses, to which we added our tithe. Then borrowing on my life insurance and asking for the return of my donation, I purchased a used car.

So began the long-planned distribution of literature and sales of Bibles in the villages of the beautiful Anahuac Valley. Over fifty villages were visited and the tracts and Gospel portions were eagerly received.

On one occasion I stopped by a canal. A young man on the far side of the canal, fearful that he might not have the time to run to the nearest bridge, took a running jump, fell just short of the bank and landed in the water. The crowd around the car was greatly amused. The young man, dripping wet, climbed up the bank of the canal and hurried to the side of the car.

"Last week you gave me some literature and I would like to have some more," he explained.

"You deserve more," I replied laughingly, "if you think it is worth getting sopping wet."

"I was afraid you might drive on before I could run to the nearest bridge, so I took a chance. I'll soon dry out," he volunteered cheerfully and the crowd joined in sympathetic laughter. They watched while I then passed him a sample of everything I had in the car. Because of his interest, the others who had been hanging back now came up to the car and began to request literature. The demand was so great that my supply was soon exhausted, and we then drove home, rejoicing in the unusual interest shown in having God's Word.

"Today we have had a wonderful time!" I exclaimed to Geraldine when I reached home. "The people's desire for my literature is almost unbelievable. The Lord is fulfilling His promise."

"I wonder what is coming next?" she replied. "Because I do not believe that the promise God gave to us is fulfilled in what is happening now."

"You don't?" I exclaimed. "Why not?"

"Because we were promised 'paths that you have not known.' What you have been doing here, up to now, is colportage work," she answered, "and you used colporters in Oaxaca. So this work is not something 'unknown.'"

And she was right!

7

A FANTASTIC FULFILLMENT

"We have covered the roads in the valley. This afternoon let us try the Cuernavaca Highway. This being Sunday, there ought to be plenty of people in the villages," I said to my companion, John Dale, who was in the city for a few days and had been invited to accompany me.

"That seems a good move. Let's do it."

Soon we were beyond Tlalpan and had begun to climb. The broad highway that is used today was not in existence then. The old road was narrow and climbed upward by numberless curves until it reached an altitude of over 10,000 feet before descending into the valley beyond.

We had driven only a few miles when we saw an army outpost. Six or eight soldiers were sitting on a bench in front of the crude huts which formed the camp. I felt a sudden urge to give literature to them.

"John, hop out of the car and give these men some literature," I suggested, "while I try and find a place to get the car off this narrow road." He did so and even before I had parked the car, he was back.

"They were eager to have the literature, Norm. And they even wanted me to explain it. They were very cordial."

"Let us see how many army camps there are this side of the summit," I suggested, and we continued to climb the winding road. Soon another outpost came into view and we found a good place to park our car. Then together we climbed the narrow path to the cluster of huts.

A number of soldiers were lounging around the camp and among them a captain. Knowing that he must be in charge of the outposts, we approached him immediately.

"It is a pleasure to meet you, captain," I said and introduced John and myself. "We have some very interesting literature which we would like to give to your men. It will give them something worthwhile to read when they are not on patrol duty. Let me show you." And I handed him a Gospel portion.

"If the men would like to have the literature, I have no objection," he replied. And we went among the men distributing the booklets. When we had finished, I returned to the captain and asked his permission to visit other camps.

"Captain, I would like to give you a copy of the New Testament. It is the last part of the Bible and I think you will find it helpful." There was veiled sarcasm in his rather profuse thanks and I realized that it had been a mistake to suggest that he might be helped through reading it. However, we parted in a friendly manner with his permission to visit other camps.

That afternoon, as we stopped at ten more outposts, we learned that there were camps every three or four miles all the way to Cuernavaca. We also discovered that the soldiers had been taught to read when they joined the army and that there was a dearth of reading material in every outpost.

At that time the soldiers of the Mexican Army were being used as rural police to make the roads safe for travel. So the camps were only temporary affairs, constructed of the materials at hand. Where rocks were plentiful, these were used to build the walls. If rocks were scarce, poles were placed in the ground a couple of feet apart and boughs woven in between them. The sides were then plastered with mud. At higher altitudes, the roofs were thatched with grass from mountain meadows. In the hot country, where palms were plentiful, their leaves were used as thatch. In a few places more permanent structures had been built during the revolutions. Most of these had parapets enclosing them.

The urge I had felt to reach these soldiers with God's Word had been growing with each outpost visited, until at the end of the afternoon I was convinced that God was guiding. Arriving home, I hurried into the house.

"God has guided in a remarkable way this afternoon, dear," I said to Geraldine the moment I saw her. "And I believe that He has shown us 'the paths that you have not known' mentioned in the promise He gave us." And we related what had happened that afternoon.

Anxious as I was to get back to that highway, it was several days before I was able to do so. On this occasion one of the Mexican pastors, Apolonio Vasquez, accompanied

A Fantastic Fulfillment

me. We decided to start where I had left off the previous Sunday.

Leaving the valley, we climbed steadily around numberless curves until at nearly 10,000 feet we came to a wide plateau. In the distance the peaks could be seen rising several thousand feet higher. Crossing the plateau, again we were in the midst of rugged mountains which towered high above us. We entered a narrow pass where the tops of the crags were wreathed in mist. It was a wild spot, made more so by the cold wind and heavy clouds. Then the narrow gorge widened and the mountain sides were less perpendicular. Here, high above the roadway, we spotted the outpost we had been told about. From their eyrie the soldiers commanded a view of the highway for several miles. The wind, bottled up by the gorge, seemed to strike this spot with increased force.

As we parked the car, no one was in sight. A lone eagle soared high above us. Slowly climbing the steep mountainside, we reached the stockade which surrounded the outpost. No one came out to meet us but a number of heads appeared above the barricade. Not a word of welcome was given, a strange thing in Mexico where courtesy is proverbial and especially in view of the cordiality of the soldiers in other outposts. The wind was cold, but it was nothing compared to our reception as I pushed open the gate and entered the enclosure. The soldiers stood around wrapped in their *zarapes* with only their eyes appearing above their mufflers. To our greeting, *"Buenos dias,"* there was no reply.

"Yes, these are the men I told you about," said one soldier to his companions; and turning to us he growled. "We don't want any of your literature."

The next couple of soldiers also refused the proffered booklet by simply remaining wrapped in their blankets.

"You will find the booklet interesting andhelpful," I said. "It tells of God's love and how He can save us from condemnation." Still no one spoke, but several of the men accepted the Gospel portions and began to look them over. A ring formed around us, and directing our words to the few who had taken the booklets, we tried to break their stony silence. The hostile attitude remained unchanged. If I had allowed myself, I could easily have thought of unpleasant things that might happen to us in this isolated spot, but I was too busy asking the Lord to intervene. And He did!

"Here comes the captain," suddenly exclaimed one of the men who was standing near the parapet. Looking over the stockade, I saw three officers begin to climb the mountainside.

"Let's go down and meet them," I said to Don Apolonio. As we approached I saw that one was a major, the second the captain to whom we had given the New Testament on our earlier visit. The third was a lieutenant. We met them about halfway up the steep climb.

"Good morning, my major," I said, using the pronoun in their customary manner to recognize his authority. "We would like to have your permission to give this literature to your men in this camp. These booklets are part of the Bible. The captain can tell you about it because I gave him some last Sunday." This was just a shot at random in the hope that the captain had read what we had given him.

"It is good! I gave permission for them to distribute it to our men in the lower camps." His cordial response surprised me, for I recalled his exaggerated thanks when we gave him the New Testament. What had caused the change I was not to learn until later.

"Yes, indeed you may," responded the major in a most friendly way. "Have you given it to the men here?"

"Only to a very few. We saw you coming and felt we should ask your permission."

"Well, come up with us now," and as we entered the stockade he ordered the sergeant, "Have the men form ranks."

"These men have some good literature which they very kindly are giving to us. Take it and read it," said the major.

We went down the line, but passed by the fanatic who had opposed us, not wishing to force it upon him. The sergeant gave orders to break ranks and the men crowded around us asking questions. The change in their attitude was nothing less than miraculous.

When the major had finished his inspection of the camp, presuming that he would likely be going to other camps, I put my car "at his orders." After inquiring which way we were going, which of course was his, he accepted the offer. With hearts full of thanksgiving and wonder at God's way of working, we descended to the car. At the next camp, the major had the men form ranks and again strongly recommended that they all read the literature. The officers and the sergeant went off to inspect the camp, giving us an opportunity to speak to the men.

The major then told us that this was the end of his command, but that he would like to inspect a section of the road that was under construction, a kilometer or two farther. We offered to drive him back to Tlalpan, where his headquarters were located, after he had seen the road

A Fantastic Fulfillment

construction ahead. Whereupon he suggested that, while he made this inspection, we drive on to the next camp. This we did and although the camp was not part of the Major's command, when we told the soldiers what we had done in other camps, they received the literature gladly. We promised to return.

In less than half an hour we were back for the major and the other officers. As we returned, the major told us that many new soldiers had moved into the camps we had visited the previous Sunday and asked us to stop in all twelve so that all his men might have the literature. This sudden turn of events left us almost breathless. To have a senior officer strongly recommend to each group of men that they carefully read the literature was more than we could have hoped for.

When halfway back to Tlalpan, the junior officers left us after giving a cordial invitation to return soon. As we approached a specially dangerous part of the road where it descended steeply and had a sharp curve, the major asked me to stop for a moment. He wanted to inspect a wrecked truck in which two men had been killed the previous day. I stopped the car where he indicated and we walked over to the edge of the ravine. There below us lay the wreck and the "pulque" barrels, with which it was loaded, lay scattered along the ravine, battered and broken. It did not surprise me that two men had been killed. We stood in silence taking in the scene.

"You will be surprised to learn," said the major, breaking the silence, "that the captain, who was with us, was on that truck. How he escaped with his life is a marvel." Here was the explanation of the captain's change of attitude. He could not help but think seriously after such a narrow escape. I was thankful that before he left us I had pressed him to take more literature.

As we travelled down the last stretch of road, our hearts, which were already overflowing with joy and thanksgiving at the way God had worked, were given further reason for rejoicing. When we approached the barracks at Tlalpan, the major invited us to come at a certain hour and give our literature to the troops there. While we were trying to thank him, he added that he had men at Xochimilco and Contreras, implying that we could go there, too. As he left us I saw sticking out of his back pocket a copy of the Spanish edition of "The Way to God," by D. L. Moody. In his breast pocket I knew he had a New Testament and some tracts. He was carrying with him all the literature we had given him.

It had been such an amazing day that I could hardly wait until I reached home to relate to Geraldine all that had happened.

"Our experiences today convince me that you were right," I said the moment I saw her. "The colportage work was not a new path, but today I believe we have found it. Remarkable opportunities to work among the Mexican soldiers have been given to us today. This I believe will prove to be the 'paths that they have not known,' which were promised to us." And I related all that had taken place.

After we had talked over all the details and marvelled at them, a thought came to mind and I exclaimed, "Without doubt this is the new work God has for me, but the amazing thing is that it should be among soldiers. I failed God during the years I was in the army. Can it be that in doing this He is fulfilling another promise? 'I will restore unto you the years that the locust hath eaten....and ye shall...be satisfied.' (Joel 2:25, 26) I believe that time will prove that this is true. God loves to be gracious."

Within the next few days we were able to visit the places mentioned by Major Garcia, so that all his men had literature. We did not see him again at this time. However, several years later I learned that he was ill in the military hospital in Mexico City and visited him. After explaining who I was and reminding him of his kindness in giving us the first opportunity to work among the soldiers I was happy to learn that his superior officers had spoken well of our work.

Suddenly he reached to the bedside table and picked up a New Testament. It looked worn and well read. "This is the New Testament you gave me that day we met on the highway. I have continued to read it almost daily."

How just and fair God is! It was only right that the man who first gave me the opportunity to work among the Mexican military should himself find Christ.

That was the beginning of opportunities that seemed almost too good to be true.

8

TOO GOOD
TO BE TRUE

"Over thirty outposts have been visited since we began this work three weeks ago," I said to Geraldine one morning at breakfast. "I promised to come back and explain the literature. If we don't do it soon, there is the chance that the soldiers will be transferred back to their barracks before we can preach in all those camps."
"You don't have classes tomorrow," Geraldine replied. "Why not invite Don Apolonio to accompany you?"
"I have delayed going back because I must prepare some kind of an object lesson to help make the message clear and to draw the men together. A chart which can be hung on the side of a hut would be best."

Some paints and other materials soon were spread on the dining room table and work began on the first of several charts which were to serve for many years in our preaching.

Something was needed to make the way of salvation simple and plain. After making a number of sketches, it came to me that an illustration of the broad and narrow ways spoken of by Jesus, might be the simplest and best. A large Y was drawn horizontally across the chart. A double line along the lower part indicated the broad way. The figure of a man was placed on each of the three sections of the road, two of them heavily laden with a burden marked "sin." A cross was put at the division of the roads, at the foot of which lay the burden of the man on the upward way. Appropriate Bible verses were added to make the message clear.

It was late that night before the chart was finished but it was ready for our adventure next day. Although I did not know it at the time, I had been led to adopt a method of

The Chart of THE BROAD AND NARROW WAYS

Too Good to Be True 63

preaching which kept us from breaking one of the religious laws of Mexico. No religious services were permitted in the open air; all had to be conducted within a building. However, by using charts in giving the message, I was not preaching but giving a *conferencia*, and this was permitted anywhere.

The next day Don Apolonio and I set out for the camps on the Cuernavaca Highway. The men gave us a very cordial welcome and even chided us a little for having delayed so long in returning.

"How many of you have read the booklets?" I asked, and from the chorus of replies I judged that some had read the gospel portions several times. I hung the chart on the side of one of the huts by pushing a stick into the heavy thatch. The men gathered closely around to read the Bible verses.

"This drawing represents life as a roadway along which everyone, without exception, is traveling. All of us are somewhere on this road, and whether we like it or not, are on the way to one of two destinations. One of these three men represents each one of us here at this moment, as God sees us. The man on the left is carrying a load on his back. What is it?"

"It is a load of sin," they answered. Then one soldier added, "But we don't carry them in a sack!"

"Right!" I answered quickly. "Where and how do we carry them?"

"On our conscience or in our hearts," several replied together.

"But the second man, who is on the narrow road upward, has no load. How did he get rid of it?"

"The load of sin is lying at the foot of the cross. So he must have gotten rid of it there," spoke up one of the men.

"Correct! The Lord Jesus Christ came to save us from our sins. That is why He died on the cross! Saint Peter wrote, 'Christ suffered for us....Who His own self bare our sins in His own body on the tree...' (I Peter 2:24) and Saint John wrote, quoting the Lord Jesus, 'He that heareth my word and believeth on Him that sent me, hath everlasting life, and shall not come into condemnation but is passed from death unto life.' (John 5:24) And here is another wonderful promise," I said, pointing to it on the chart. "'As many as received him (Christ) to them gave He power to become sons of God, even to them that believe on His name.'" (John 1:12)

"Now let us look at this man who is on the narrow upward way. How is he different from the other two men?" I asked.

"He has lost his burden of sins," said one.

"He has been forgiven by Christ. And that is why he has a smile on his face," suggested another.

"How about this last verse I read to you from the charts? What is he now? What great change has taken place?" I said, pressing the point.

The men drew nearer to the chart and then one exclaimed, "He is made a son of God!" and there seemed to be a sense of awe in his tone of voice. "Imagine being a son of God!"

"How did he get all these things?" They remained silent. It seemed as though God's truth was almost too good to believe, and I decided to help them a little.

"There is a verse in the Bible which says, 'The wages of sin is death,'" and I paused and pointed to the man on the downward path who still carried his load of sin. Then I added, "But the gift of God is eternal life through Jesus Christ our Lord." (Romans 6:23)

"Then it is a gift!" several exclaimed in unison.

"That is exactly what God's Word says. What do you have to do to receive a gift? For instance, what do you have to do to accept this gift?" and I extended a booklet.

"Reach out and take it and say 'thank you,'" replied one and smiled as he took the proferred booklet. "Is it that simple?"

Then we reviewed all the blessings which this man had received as a gift, adding eternal life to those already mentioned.

"Why is this other man on the downward road?" I asked and the answer came almost in a chorus!

"He did not receive Jesus as Savior;" "He did not believe!" "He refused God's gift;" and other opinions, more or less the same were given.

"Do any of you want to follow that road?"

"No, indeed!" was the unanimous reply.

"Then what must each one do to be on the upward road?"

"Believe on the Lord Jesus Christ!" responded one. "Receive God's gift!" said another.

"The Bible says, 'Believe on the Lord Jesus Christ, and thou shalt be saved.' (Act 16:31). How many of you believe that He died for you and will receive Him as your personal Savior? If you will, raise your hands, but only do so if you truly want Him to come into your hearts and give you a new kind of life."

Every hand was raised. Then followed an explanation of what they should do to live like children of God: Read God's Word, come to God as a father telling Him the needs

Too Good to Be True

of each day, and then tell others of what Christ had done for them.

The thought that God is a heavenly Father seemed to strike them with special force. That, like a human father, He was interested in every phase of their lives, seemed almost too good to be true. When the promise, "Call upon Me and I will answer you" (Jeremiah 33:3) was quoted and shown to be in the Bible, they began to realize their privileges as sons of God.

"Remember God loves to answer our prayers," I reminded them, "and to encourage us to pray has filled His Word with many promises, like the one I mentioned. When you come across one in the Bible, mark it. When it meets a need, ask God to fulfill His promises. He will not fail!"

Then Bibles and New Testaments were offered for sale and many were purchased. Of course the price was far below cost, but experience had taught us that books were valued more and taken better care of if something was paid for them. Only Gospel portions and tracts were given away.

Over the years this scene was repeated in hundreds of barracks and outposts in different parts of Mexico. The response of the men varied from group to group, but the message was the same, the simple presentation of God's Love and Grace. It almost always resulted in some soldiers committing themselves to the Lord. The follow-up work convinced us that in most cases the decision was genuine.

Every time this first chart was used, we tried to make it very clear that the decision they were asked to make was a personal matter between each individual and God, that Christ had said, "Behold I stand at the door (of the heart) and knock; if any man hear my voice, and open the door, I will come in to him..." (Revelation 3:20). In fulfillment of that promise He comes into the one who believes and gives new life.

It was a constant joy to see how many of the men tried seriously to follow our suggestions and, as a result, did grow spiritually. The change in the lives of the soldiers was so evident that a general said, "Please visit my regiment as often as possible, because the men who accept your teaching are more conscientious and faithful than others in carying out their duties."

Frequently I had to recognize that, before we had a chance to preach, men had been led to the Lord and decisions had been made as a result of the simple reading of God's Word. For that reason, I always tried to visit a camp and distribute Gospel portions some days before giving any explanation. We are told, "The Word of God is living and active, sharper than any two-edged sword, piercing even to the dividing asunder of soul and spirit...and is a discerner of the thoughts and intents of the heart." (Hebrews 4:12). We saw this promise fulfilled innumerable times.

There was the case of a hard-boiled sergeant who was anything but pleased when we visited his camp and told him that his senior officer had given permission to us to distribute literature to his men.

"We don't want anything religious here," he growled when he saw the Gospel portion marked "St. Luke."

"The captain gave permission," I replied.

"During the revolution I strung up fourteen priests," he boasted, as we started to distribute literature.

"God can forgive you for that and all your other sins through Christ, if you ask Him," I replied.

"What is this literature?" he asked.

"These booklets are portions of the Bible and they show that God loves us in spite of all the wrong we may have done. Read it, sergeant! It can't do you any harm." And he accepted a portion as well as a pamphlet which made plain the way of salvation.

A few days later, when we returned to that outpost the sergeant saw us parking the car and hurried down to meet us, book in hand.

"This is God's truth, *senores*," he exclaimed even before he greeted us.

Week after week we saw evidences of the working of the Holy Spirit in the hearts of the men and were reminded of Christ's words and His promise, "You have not chosen me, but I have chosen you, and ordained you, that you go and bring forth fruit, and that your fruit shall remain." (John 15:16)

Such a promise caused me to be constantly alert for the opportunities He provided and made each day truly an adventure with God.

One day I was traveling on the international highway toward Mexico City but was still several hours away when I saw a captain standing at a bus stop. I pulled over and stopped the car.

"Can I give you a lift, captain? I am going all the way through the city."

"Thank you. That is where I have to go," he replied. I opened the door, he jumped in beside me, and we swung back on the highway.

"This booklet might interest you. Look it over as we drive." I handed him a New Testament. Out of the corner of my eye, I watched him thumb through the book, stopping in a few places to read a verse or two. Evidently he saw

Too Good to Be True

the names of the Gospels, because he finally closed the book and turned to me.

"I don't believe in the saints!" and laid down the book in a manner that was to lead me to understand that this was the beginning and end of our conversation on this subject.

"Nor do I!" I replied, and said nothing more. There was a puzzled silence.

"I don't believe in the Virgin Mary," he said with increased emphasis.

Knowing that he meant he did not worship her, I again replied, "Nor do I!" And there was an even longer silence.

Finally he spoke again. "I don't believe in the priests and their confessionals."

To which I again replied, "Nor do I!"

His reaction was immediate: "If you don't believe in these things, in what do you believe?"

This was exactly what I was jockeying for, and I began to explain the Gospel to him. We were in a very mountainous part and so at the first wide spot we pulled off the road. Using the New Testament, which he now had in his hand, we began to look up and read passages about salvation. He asked many questions, and as far as possible, I had him read the answers from the Scriptures. I have no idea how long we talked, but finally he exclaimed, "I have always believed that if there is a God, He would have a religion such as you describe. What must I do to join?"

"Jesus Christ did not come to found a new religion, but to give us life through faith in Him. Look what He Himself said," and I opened the New Testament at John, chapter ten, and pointed to the last part of verse ten.

He read aloud, "I am come that they may have life, and that they might have it more abundantly."

"Turn back several pages to chapter five and read verse twenty-four," I suggested, and in a moment he had found the place.

"Verily, verily, I say unto you, he that heareth my Word and believeth..." He stopped reading and asked, "Who is speaking?"

"Look at the nineteenth verse."

"It is Jesus!" he said in surprise, and then continued to read the rest of the verse. "He that believeth...hath everlasting life and shall not come into judgment, but is passed from death unto life."

"How simple and yet how wonderful!" he said after a moment of silence.

"All you have to do is to ask Jesus to come into your life, forgive your sins, and give you everlasting life. And he will do it."

"How do you speak to Him?" he asked.

"He is here with us at this very moment. We can talk to Him as to a friend who might be in the car with us. Repeat this simple prayer after me and you will feel in your heart that He has heard." We bowed our heads and he repeated a short prayer, asking Christ to come into his heart. After we had finished, we were silent for a few minutes.

Then he exclaimed, "How good God is!"

As we drove along, we talked of the Christian life and what one must do to develop our spiritual lives. I dropped him at his destination and commended him to the Lord. I never saw him again, but believe I will some day.

However, I did see hundreds of other military men make similar decisions with life changing results.

9

BETTER THAN EXPECTED

"It is a real joy to have you with me today, Fritz. I am so glad that you phoned offering to accompany me." This I said to F. J. Huegel as we drove toward the Cuernavaca Highway, where I planned to visit outposts.

"Not at all! When I heard of this work you are doing among the Mexican military, I was interested at once," he replied. "You will recall that I served as chaplain with the American forces. It seems to me that God is working in a very unusual way. What you are doing deserves the support of all of us."

It was encouraging to hear his estimate of this work, because I had a high regard for his opinion on spiritual matters. I had known him for a number of years and had been greatly helped by reading one of his books, *Bone of His Bone*. It is a remarkable exposition of our union with Christ and came out of a very tragic personal experience. He was living in one of the northern cities of Mexico and was holding evangelistic services in a local theater. He had received threatening letters, warning that if the services were continued something would happen to him or his family. After praying about it, he felt led to continue the meetings. One day their little three-year-old daughter became desperately ill. When she was rushed to the hospital, the doctors found that someone had given the child poisoned candy, but it was too late to save her life. Out of the agonizing "Why?" which followed this experience grew this book, which has blessed thousands. Just recently the Huegels had moved to Mexico City and he was teaching in the Union Theological Seminary.

"How do you account for this unusual opportunity among the military?" Fritz asked. "It has never been done before."

"It is the Spirit of God working. There is no other explanation. However, God gave me a promise when I was ill and discouraged that He would lead me in paths that were not known. The promise is being fulfilled in what we are experiencing."

"Yes, but are there providential preparations which you can see?" he inquired.

"There are a number. For instance, that troops should be used as rural police on the new and improved highways is one. Also, that the men who could not read when they joined the army have been taught how. Here they are isolated in these outposts for two or three months with little to do when off patrols. It is not surprising that they welcome our literature and read it several times before we can return. It would be hard to find a more ideal situation!" I said with enthusiasm.

"You are right about the men, but how do you account for the officers' readiness to let you do this evangelistic work among their men?"

"The Lord has cared for that as well. Most of the senior officers and some of the junior ones are Masons and as Masons, they accept the Bible. I always explain that the portions I am distributing are part of the Bible. Also, many of the officers are anticlerical. They have not forgotten the recent *Cristero* revolution which followed the promulgation of the new religious laws. Although it was suppressed, the army suffered heavy casualties. However, I never refer to the differences in religions, but simply give them the Gospel and they recognize it as a clarification of truths they already know."

"While we are speaking of the providence of God," I continued, "you will be interested to learn that without knowing the restrictions imposed by the new religious laws, I was led to use charts when preaching in the camps. This makes the sermon a conference, which is permitted anywhere."

"I wondered about that," Fritz replied, "because I learned the hard way that now no street meetings are permitted. All religious services must be held in churches."

"My first chart was of The Two Ways, but I have just prepared another, which I call The Three Crosses. It is an explanation of the crucifixion scene and the repentant thief," I explained. "This new chart emphasizes the two groups in the world: those who accept Christ and those who reject Him. There are Bible verses written on the chart,

Better Than Expected

so you won't have any difficulty using it, but don't feel bound to follow it. It helps to use eye-gate as well as ear-gate but, as I have mentioned, the main reason for its use is it keeps us within the law."

"I think it remarkable that you were led so clearly to avoid any conflict with the law. Furthermore, it is good sermonizing to use things to illustrate truth. It holds people's attention and clarifies points. I will be happy to use this chart," he responded.

I had told Fritz when we started out that it was a joy to have him with me and, as the day progressed, it proved to be that and more. He fit in perfectly and seemed to sense the attitude of the different groups as we went from camp to camp. His Spanish was beautiful and he made the story of the repentant thief live to the listening men. "Look and live" became a present reality to the listeners and demanded a response. It was not surprising that in the camps the men who had made decisions on a previous visit reaffirmed them and that others, who had been absent on patrols when we had made our earlier visit, joined their comrades in their decision to follow Christ.

"The response of the men so far has been thrilling," Fritz remarked as we left the third camp.

"Wait until you meet the men in the outpost at kilometer 34," I responded. "They are the ones who always give me a boost. Sergeant Martinez is a dedicated man and constantly helps and encourages his men to be faithful. You will enjoy them," I assured him.

When we reached kilometer 34, the soldiers came down to meet us and crowded around the car. When I produced the chart we were to use, Sergeant Martinez took it from me and after climbing the bank to the camp, he led us past all the huts to one that was brand new. Opening the door, he ushered us in and the men followed. Imagine our surprise! They had constructed a little chapel and on the walls were two roughly made texts, "God is Love" and "Christ, the Prince of Peace." We were almost overwhelmed by this evidence of the sincerity of the men. The rough benches they had made would seat about fifteen people.

"Sergeant, this is really wonderful and we congratulate you on having made it," I said when I could get my emotions under control. "How do you use it?"

"We gather here once a day and read a passage from the Bible and discuss it," replied the sergeant. "Also, the men come here to be quiet when they want to do their own reading."

At that time the Mexican army had no commissary department and so the wives and children accompanied the men when they moved to the outposts. Food was bought by the women in the nearest village. When we spoke in the camps, usually some of the women listened from a distance, but I noticed that now only the soldiers were present.

"Sergeant, I have a special treat for you today. My companion gave *conferencias* to the soldiers in Europe during the Great World War and will speak to us using this new chart. Why not invite the women and children to come and listen?"

In a few minutes the place was packed and all listened with intense interest to Fritz's message. At the end, all reaffirmed their faith in Christ and I reminded them as usual that they were now children of God, that God was their heavenly Father and ready to help them in every need.

"To encourage us to pray, God has given us many promises in the Bible and there is one in the eleventh chapter of the Gospel of Matthew, verse twenty-eight, that you ought to memorize: 'Come unto me, all ye that labour and are heavy laden, and I will give you rest.' Who is speaking?"

"Jesus Christ," responded several who had their Bibles open.

"Yes! It is Jesus Christ Himself who has made this promise. And to help us understand how this is possible, he uses an illustration which all of us can understand. When Jesus lived in Palestine, they must have had a custom very similar to one that you have here in Mexico," I said to arouse their interest.

"How many of you have seen a young ox broken in to pull a plough?" I asked, and even some of the women nodded. "What is the first thing you do?"

"Fasten the yoke to the horns of the old ox," said several.

"Then what do you do?" I asked.

"Put the other end of the yoke on the young ox and lash it to its horns," they replied.

"Does the young ox like it?"

"No indeed! It tries to run away but can't. The yoke twists its head one way and then another. It finds that bucking can do no good," were among the answers which came from the men.

"Where is the tongue of the plough or sled tied?"

"To the yoke beam, right up against the old ox," they replied.

"Right. Then which ox is carrying the whole load?"

"The old one," was the answer without a dissenting voice.

"What does the young ox have to learn in order to keep the yoke from grinding against its horns?" I asked.

Better Than Expected

"To walk with the old ox," said one. "To keep in step," suggested another.

"Now listen to what the Lord Jesus says, 'Take my yoke upon you and learn of me....For my yoke is easy and my burden is light.' How can it be easy and light?" I inquired.

"He bears the heavy end," came the prompt reply.

"What are we to learn from this?" I asked.

"To be obedient." "To do His will." "To walk with Him," were among the answers showing that they understood the illustration.

"And if we do this, what are we promised?" I said to press the point home.

"That He will carry our burdens and give us rest," they replied.

"Remember this truth each day as you ask Him in prayer to be with you and to help in every problem that comes," I added.

We had such a good time with these men that we were reluctant to leave, but the hour was late and it was beginning to get dark.

"This has been a wonderful day, Norm," Fritz volunteered as we drove home. "I have one free day each week in my teaching. If I may, I would like to come out with you on that day."

"If you may!" I exclaimed. "Nothing could please me more."

This was the beginning of a partnership which was to last as long as the soldier work continued, and a friendship which continued until Fritz was called into the Lord's presence. For well over a decade we were prayer partners and met as frequently as possible to pray for his and my responsibilities in our mission work.

A month or two after Fritz had begun to accompany me regularly once a week, we were on the Cuernavaca Highway and stopped at a camp. The men had been reading the Gospel portions for about ten days and were eager to have an explanation.

I had asked Fritz to give the message, and as he spoke I leaned against one of the huts. Suddenly my attention was caught by a moan which seemed to come from within. I listened intently and heard it again. Then there came a cry of pain. I was distressed and moved toward the group of soldiers. Fortunately, Fritz was just completing his message and was driving home the truth that God, through Christ, becomes our heavenly Father and will hear and answer prayer.

"Excuse me, Fritz," I said as he finished. "I would like to ask the men who is ill in this house," indicating the one where I had been standing.

"It is my wife, *señores*," replied the sergeant. "She is very ill. Would you pray for her?"

"Yes, indeed!" Fritz replied. "What is her trouble?"

"She suffered a miscarriage," replied the sergeant, "and she has a very high fever. She is too ill to move to the hospital." As he spoke he pushed open the door of the hut for us to enter. One glance at the woman showed that she was desperately ill.

Responding to the request of the sergeant, we both prayed for his wife and one or perhaps both of us used Bible promises as a basis for our requests. When we were finished, Fritz reminded the sergeant that he, too, could pray for his wife's recovery.

"I wish we could get a doctor to see this poor woman," I remarked as we left the hut.

"It is possible that Doctora Baez might be willing to come," Fritz answered. "Suppose we drive back to Tlalpan and I can telephone her and see if she could."

This we did, and Dr. Baez said she could be ready by the time we reached her office in the center of the city. In an hour and a half we were back at the outpost and the doctor went into the hut. It was some time before she came out and approaching us, spoke in a low voice.

"She is in very bad shape, has peritonitis, and even if we had her in the hospital, I doubt that she could recover. However, I have done what I could, and if you will bring me, I will come back tomorrow and see her again."

"Sergeant, the *doctora* has offered to return tomorrow and I will bring her." With his thanks ringing in our ears, we left the encampment.

Before noon the next day we were back and were very thankful to learn from the sergeant that his wife was resting quietly. The doctor went into the hut. When she finally came out, she was smiling and reported so that all could hear.

"Sergeant, your wife's condition has improved. If this continues, I would like to see her in my office in a week or ten days. Sr. Taylor will keep me informed on her condition."

The wife continued to improve and in a little over a week, she felt well enough to make the trip into town. I made an appointment and drove her to the doctor's office. As we left the office, the doctor said to me, "This is nothing less than a miracle! When I saw her the first time, I thought the case seemed hopeless."

Better Than Expected 75

Arriving back in the camp, I repeated the doctor's remarks to the sergeant and to my surprise he replied in a most matter-of-fact tone of voice, "Of course it is a miracle! Ever since I learned that through Christ God becomes our heavenly Father, I have been asking Him day and night to make my wife well again. He has promised to hear and answer our requests. When He works, it is a miracle."

Later, when at home, I phoned Fritz to tell him the outcome of the matter and I quoted the sergeant's words.

"If every believer had such child-like faith, we would be seeing continuous miracles, for God loves to hear and answer prayer," he replied.

"Yes, and Christ would be the living reality he longs to be to every Christian." I hung up the phone and as I joined Geraldine in front of the fire in the living room, I repeated Fritz's comment.

"I think you are seeing more examples of this child-like faith among the soldier converts than you realize," she replied.

"What men are you referring to?"

"How about the corporal whose horse stumbled, threw him, and the whole troop rode over him. In that moment he cried out to God and was unharmed. Before all his comrades he attributed his escape to God's loving care. That is child-like faith! He could have said it was just good luck. And how about the soldier's wife who lost a chicken and asked all the others in the camp to pray that a coyote had not gotten it. On your next visit to the camp she told the story and finished with the words, 'The next night when I went to shut the chicken coop, it was back with the rest. Where it had been that night no one knows.' The others in the camp said that they too had prayed when she asked them to. Isn't that child-like faith?"

"You are right!" I agreed. "The converts among the soldiers have shown remarkable faith. When they ask God for something they just expect to see their prayers answered because, through Christ, they are His children. Their belief in God's love is something beautiful." We sat quietly before the fire thinking of these experiences which God had given us when suddenly a thought came to me.

"Did I ever tell you of the sequel to Corporal Garcia's experience of falling off his horse? I mean his wife's experience?"

"Not that I recall. It may have happened while I was away."

"It is really more remarkable than the husband's experience. They were on the Puebla Highway and the wife had gone to a hearby village to buy supplies. She had returned and was climbing the pathway to the camp when suddenly the whole front of their hut burst into flames. She cried out to God for help, dropped her bundle, and rushed up the pathway and tried to beat out the flames with her shawl. At that very instant a truckload of road workers drove up, stopped, and all the men with their shovels joined her and soon the fire was out. Only the front of the hut was destroyed and nothing of value was lost. She saw it as a double miracle. First, that the thatch must have smouldered since breakfast was prepared, and only burst into flame at the moment she returned. The second was the arrival of the road workers at the crucial moment. She told us all that since her husband's escape from injury when the troop rode over him, she has believed in prayer. Now she knows that God not only answers prayer, but is constantly watching over those who trust Him."

Again we sat quietly for a time just watching the open fire. Then Geraldine summed up our thoughts.

"We speak of child-like faith, but actually it is simply believing that God keeps His promises. We make our requests and, with expectancy, we watch to see how and where He will work."

"You're right! It's as simple as that!"

Within a few weeks we were to have another example from a most unexpected source.

10

ADVENTURING WITH GOD

"Dad! Mr. Huegel wants to speak to you on the phone," called my daughter, Joy. "He says he has almost unbelievable news for you."

I hurried to the phone. "Hello, Fritz. What is the good news? I'm curious to know."

"I still can hardly believe it is true!" he replied. "After the service this morning at Gante Methodist Church, I met a high-ranking Mexican army officer who was converted ten days ago. I told him of your work and he wants to meet you."

"It is almost too good to be true. Who is he? How did it happen?"

"He is Colonel Rodolfo Curti and, until recently, he was head of the Mexico City Traffic Department. And this you will find hard to believe, Norm. He was brought to the Lord through a dream."

"A dream!" I exclaimed. "You're kidding me!"

"No, it is an actual fact. He had this dream and was so disturbed that he came to the midweek service and accepted the Lord. What is more, he is on fire for the Lord."

"When can I meet him?"

"He has invited us to come to his home tomorrow afternoon. Can you make it?"

"Of course! I can hardly wait for the time to come," I told him. "To me, this is just a further development of the Lord's promise. 'I will lead them in paths that they have not known.' It is difficult for us to do any work with the higher officers. All I have done so far is to give them Bibles and New Testaments, so perhaps God has raised up this man to evangelize the higher ranks of the military."

The following afternoon I picked up Fritz at his home and soon we were at the colonel's residence, for he lived on our side of the city. The colonel opened the door. He was a dark, heavyset man of about average height with a friendly, open smile. Yet one sensed strength of character. Here was a man who was accustomed to making decisions and being obeyed. He greeted us both with a Mexican embrace and to my delight at once called me "Brother Taylor."

"I am anxious to hear about the work you are doing among our troops," he said, addressing me as we sat down.

"Pardon me, colonel," I answered, "but could we first hear your story, because I feel that God has called you to be a witness among the higher ranking officers."

"To help you understand my story," the colonel began, "I will have to go back some years. I was stationed in a mountain village in the state of Oaxaca and became very ill and went into a coma. The people thought I had died and laid me out for burial. I regained consciousness and soon after that a doctor who had been sent out from Oaxaca City arrived. He wanted to take me there for an operation, but felt that I could only stand the trip if there were ice compresses on my abdomen. While waiting for ice to be sent from the city, hailstones as big as eggs fell in the village. They gathered as much as they could, put me on a litter, and we started the long trek to the railway line. When I was restored to health, people spoke of the hailstones' falling in the village as a 'miracle.' I, in my unbelief, always replied, 'Nonsense! It was just a coincidence.'*

"This was my attitude. I despised all religions and so one day, when my hands had become dirty, I went into the church in front of Sanborn's and washed them in the holy water. Later, when all church property was nationalized, I was assigned the task of doing so in the Federal District. It gave me real pleasure. I am telling this simply to show how patient and loving God has been toward me. He should have struck me dead long ago for my antagonism.

"Recently, because of certain developments, I became very discouraged," he continued after a pause. "I even considered committing suicide and my wife hid my guns. Then one night about two weeks ago I had a dream. In it, I left the house and went down street after street looking for someone, whom I was not sure. I met a group of people and it was suggested that we search together. When we turned a corner, in front of us we saw a man sitting in a doorway. How I recognized Him as the Lord Jesus, I don't

---
*See note at end of chapter.

know, but I dropped on my knees before Him and the remembrance of my antagonism and ingratitude flooded my mind. At the same time, I was conscious of his love and concern for me. Bowed there before Him, I noticed that His hands and feet shone, almost like polished brass..." He paused and a look of wonder, almost awe, seemed to pass over his face as he recalled the scene.

"You say that to you it seemed as though His feet and hands shone like brass?" I asked.

"Yes, that is the only way I can describe it."

"Colonel, where have you been reading in the Bible?" I inquired.

"I have read and reread the Gospels. I want to learn all I can about Christ's ministry here on earth."

"Let me read you a verse or two from the book of Revelation," I said with a feeling of excitement. "'In the midst of the candlesticks was one like unto the Son of Man....His eyes were as a flame of fire; His feet like unto fine brass, as if they burned in a furnace.'" I paused and passed the Bible to the colonel.

"Where is this passage?" asked the colonel in surprise.

"Fourteenth and fifteenth verses of the first chapter," I replied and pointed to where he would find them on the open page.

"You truly saw the Lord in your dream," Fritz assured him.

The colonel slowly read the portion indicated and then closed the Bible and was silent. We hesitated to say anything.

"Yes, I know I saw Him," the colonel replied, breaking the silence. "I am not an emotional man but as I knelt before Him in my dream, I burst into tears and awoke crying. This awoke my wife and she exclaimed, 'What has happened?' and all I could answer was, 'I have seen Jesus Christ!' and it seemed to me that the far side of the bedroom was aglow with light.

"Finally, with difficulty, I was able to control my emotions and got dressed. I was still overwhelmed by my indifference and ingratitude toward God and had no desire to eat. I kept walking back and forth in this room. Finally I recalled where the Bible Society store was located and sent my son to buy a Bible. I read passage after passage without finding peace. Then my wife and I decided to go to the Gante Methodist Church. We arrived late and someone was giving a Bible study on the subject of sin. As she wrote one sin after another on the blackboard, I turned to my wife and remarked, 'Someone must have told her about me.' After the study was over, the pastor gave an invitation to anyone who wanted to open his heart to Christ to come forward. I responded and, as I knelt at the altar, was happy to find my wife was kneeling with me."

We were deeply moved by Colonel Curti's story and at his suggestion, Fritz led us in prayer thanking God for His goodness in revealing Himself in such a remarkable way. Also, he prayed that the Lord would guide and direct the colonel and Mrs. Curti as they sought to serve Him.

Colonel Curti was very anxious to learn all he could about the Christian life and the remainder of the afternoon was spent in answering questions and explaining Bible truths. We were surprised at his spiritual perception and the work of grace which had already been accomplished in his life. He seemed to recognize instinctively his responsibilities as a believer. Already he was deeply immersed in Bible study, was a man of prayer, and to our delight, we learned that he had begun to witness to his fellow officers.

This was the beginning of a friendship which continued over many years. We entered into an agreement to pray for each other daily and while he remained in Mexico City, we met frequently. He supported me in my work among Mexican soldiers with his interest, his prayers, and at times very valuable suggestions.

Up to this time we had been so busy visiting the outposts on the highways near at hand that we had not thought of troop concentrations in other parts of the country. One day Curti suggested that we visit Acapulco.

"A very good friend of mine, General Vicente Leon, is commander of that zone. And I am sure that he will not only allow you to distribute literature but will want you to speak to his men in the barracks. I will give you a letter of introduction."

Immediately I consulted with Fritz, because if we were to make the trip, I wanted him to come along to give the conference in the barracks. The more we both thought and prayed over the matter, the clearer it seemed that the visit should be made. Two Bible promises helped to confirm this conviction, "The steps of a good man are ordered by the Lord," (Psalm 37:23) and "The Lord shall guide thee continually..." (Isaiah 58:11).

On the highway to Acapulco there were many army outposts and so it seemed that the trip would take at least two weeks. The plan was to visit the camps on our way down, leave literature, and then on the way back speak in as many as possible. Substitutes were found for our classes in the seminaries and we were ready to go. Then a very good friend, Dr. William Ross of a sister mission, asked to join us and we were delighted to have this addition to our forces.

We planned to camp out and were pulling a little folding trailer. Upon arriving in Acapulco and inquiring about a place where we could camp, we were directed to a lovely beach and bay called La Caleta. It was a very popular place for bathers because an island sheltered the bay from heavy breakers. Many people were swimming and so we pitched our camp well back from the beach, almost against the jungle. Behind us it seemed to be a solid mass of foliage.

It was a beautiful spot and after an enjoyable swim and supper, we sat around watching the sunset. As the sun began to disappear, the clouds and water were turned to molten gold. The breakers died in golden ripples at our feet. Its beauty left us almost breathless and we sat quietyly meditating as the darkness gathered. Some people were still swimming, but it had been a long and tiring day so we decided to retire.

We had already learned that Curti had been correct in saying that there was a large concentration of troops in the area, and we looked forward to the next day with keen anticipation. We were to present Curti's letter to the commander of the zone and hoped for real opportunities. So, before going to bed, we had a time of prayer. Sitting on the beds in the little trailer, we read several passages from the Bible and then knelt in the cramped quarters. Dr. Ross and I prayed first and, conscious of the bathers who were still nearby, we prayed in low voices seeking God's guidance and blessing for the task before us.

When it came Fritz's turn to pray, he was so burdened for the soldiers we hoped to reach next day that, forgetful that the canvas sides of the trailer were not soundproof, he allowed his voice to rise higher and higher. He was utterly unconscious of anyone except the Lord to whom he was making his requests and his burden for the soldiers.

Next day we had proof that both God and man had heard his prayer.

Early the next morning we were at the barracks and almost immediately were ushered into the general's office.

"Welcome, *senores*," he said. "In what way can I serve you?"

"General, we have a letter of introduction to you from your good friend and ours, Colonel Rodolfo Curti." And I passed him the letter.

"Friends of Curti are my friends," he answered, and without taking time to read the letter, he arose from his desk, came and gave all three of us a warm Mexican *abrazo* (embrace). Then he waved us to seats as he took his place behind the desk and began to read the letter.

"I will be glad to have you give my men this literature which the colonel recommends so highly. He says it has changed his life. That is remarkable."

"It is true, General Leon. Rodolfo Curti is a changed man. He has found a relationship with God through faith in Jesus Christ."

"He was an agnostic!" exclaimed the general. "That is a change! And he says that he has a joy and peace such as he never had before."

"This is what God wants to do for all men, and we have seen many of the soldiers find that same peace and joy. That is why we want to give this literature to your men and, if you wish, we can give a conference to the men so that they can understand what the literature teaches."

"Good!" the general replied. "This evening at the hour of roll call. Meanwhile, I have a large detachment of men at La Pie de la Cuesta and, if you will take me in your car, we will go there right now and distribute the literature."

Soon we were on the way to this detachment and as we drove along the coast, the general asked many questions about Curti and the work we had done among the soldiers. Before we knew it, we were at the outpost.

"Have the men form ranks, sergeant," ordered the general. In a very few minutes about forty men were in the formation. "These men kindly have offered to give you literature which can be very helpful. I strongly recommend that you read it carefully and follow its advice. It has been given to many of your comrades in other areas and because of it they are better soldiers. This gentleman will tell you how this can happen."

Fritz explained that the portions were part of the Bible and drew their attention to the slip which was pasted on the back of the front cover giving Bible verses on salvation and an invitation to accept God's offer of salvation through Christ.

The general was very enthusiastic about what had been done and, as we dropped him at his headquarters, reminded us that he would expect us at five o'clock that afternoon.

Rejoicing in the working of God's Spirit, we returned to our camp at La Caleta and spent the afternoon enjoying the beauty of the spot.

At the appointed hour we were again at the barracks. The men were formed in a hollow square and after we had given then Gospel portions and tracts, Fritz spoke on the subject, "Jesus, the friend of soldiers," referring to the

Adventuring With God

story of the centurion and other military men touched by Christ as related in the New Testament. The general became so interested that he and his officers moved quite close so as not to miss anything that was said. Afterward they were all very profuse in their thanks and invited us to return.

We drove back to our camp full of praise and thanksgiving for the way God had answered our prayers. It seemed that He had fulfilled beyond our expectation the purpose of our coming.

But that evening we were to have an experience that showed us how God loves to answer prayer in a way "above that which we can ask or think."

He had ordered our steps and guided us as He had promised!

Note from page 78.

A few months later, we learned of another remarkable occurance. On the second day, when all the ice was exhausted, they placed the Colonel, on his litter, in the shade of a giant cactus, expecting him to die. Again heavy clouds gathered and more hail fell. This renewed supply lasted until they met the ice which had been sent from the city. The first witness was a school teacher who had been on the trip. The second was the officer who commanded the detail which carried the Colonel to the railhead. I interviewed both men. How marvellous are God's providences.

11

ONE OF THE LEAST

In the morning, after leaving General Leon at the barracks, we had returned to our camp at La Caleta to await our appointment with him in the late afternoon. Folding chairs were set up and we settled down for a quiet afternoon of reading and enjoying the beauty about us. Large trees gave us heavy shade from the tropical sun and, on the beach, children and adults frolicked in the surf. The shade and the heat had made us all sleepy and, I believe, we were dozing when we became conscious of an old Indian woman standing near.

"Good afternoon, *señora*. Is there anything we can do for you?"

"Forgive my disturbing you, *señores*, but I heard you praying last night and I think perhaps you can help me."

"You heard us praying!" one of us exclaimed. "How was that?"

"You put your tent right on the path that leads to our hut, which is just inside the bush."

"We are sorry if we blocked the entrance to your home."

"There are other paths to our hut. I am glad you put it there because it let me hear you praying and that makes me sure you can help my family and me."

"What is your need or problem?" two of us asked almost in unison.

"We are refugees here, having fled from our mountain village because evil men killed my husband and might have killed my sons if we had not left our home. We came to this far side of Acapulco because we think the police will not let those bandits enter the city. My sons support us by cutting firewood for the restaurant nearby. What we need is to know more about God."

"What do you know about the Lord Jesus Christ?" Fritz asked.

"I heard a man talk about Him once and something happened to me and I want my family to hear about Him, too."

"Tell us your experience," was the request that came from all of us.

"About six months ago I was visiting relatives here in Acapulco," she answered, "and one Sunday evening I was walking along a street and heard singing. The door was open and I stopped to listen. Someone invited me to come inside and I sat down on one of the back benches. A man was speaking about the love of God and told us that Jesus Christ loves us, too. I did not understand what he was telling us but when he asked us to go forward if we would like to have God come into our lives, I went with others." She paused and we three waited quietly for her to go on. It was clear that her emotions had been stirred by the memory of that night.

"I don't know what happened, *señores*, but a peace and joy came into my heart such as I had never known before. I returned to my village, but was afraid to tell my husband because I had learned that it was a Protestant church I had been in and I was afraid he would beat me. Then I became ill and when I was very sick I felt I should tell him what had happened. And when he heard, instead of beating me he said if it had made me happy that was fine.

"Shortly after that an old feud broke out in the village and my husband was killed. My son was threatened and we fled, taking with us only the things we could carry. We came here, because as I told you, we hope the police will not let those evil men enter the city. When we found that the restaurant needed wood, we built our little hut right back of you in the jungle. It is about three weeks since we came and we feel secure here." She puased for a moment and then, recalling her original request, added, "When can you tell my family about the love of God?"

"Bring them down right now," I answered.

"The boys are out cutting wood and will not be back until after sundown."

"Then come this evening when all the bathers have left the beach and the moon is shining. That will be fine." And the dear soul left us, profuse in her thanks.

It was growing dark when we got back from our afternoon visit to the barracks and the night noises of the jungle had already begun. Thrilled with all that had happened that day, we took time before preparing our supper to thank

God for the marvelous way He had worked among the troops. It far exceeded anything we had anticipated. With a sense of awe we watched the brilliant sunset colors slowly dying in the west, a further indication of God's almighty power.

But the real climax of the trip was to come that evening. Perhaps it was the real purpose of our coming. The beach was deserted and the moonlight almost as bright as day when the dear old Indian woman and her family appeared. There were eight in all--the old mother, the eldest son and his wife, four boys in their teens and a young daughter.

To take advantage of the light of the moon, we had them sit in a half circle near the water's edge, and I spread a chart on the sand before them. Then, turning to Fritz, I suggested, "It was your praying out loud last night that brings them here. It should be your privilege to tell them about Christ."

Taking a camp stool, he sat down in front of them and explained the way of salvation, continually referring to the chart on the sand. He asked them questions to make sure that they were grasping the truth.

The scene will always remain etched on my mind: the almost full moon above us; the distant roar of the surf which died into bright ripples near where we sat; the faces of young people seen clearly in the moonlight as they looked upward toward Fritz, listening intently to every word spoken; the face of the dear old Indian mother half hidden in shadows as she sat with slightly bowed head. And above the noise of the distant surf and the jungle night sounds, the voice of Fritz telling again, eloquently as he always could, the old, old story which is forever new.

Finally an invitation was given to the group to open their hearts to Christ and one by one they signified their desire to do so. Then Fritz turned to the mother and said, "God is like a father. When we have needs, we ask Him to supply them. Then when we receive the things we have asked for, we thank Him. Would you like to thank God that all your family now belong to Christ and are God's children?"

After a moment or two of silence that dear old soul prayed, thanking God that He had sent us to tell them of His love. I think that we three were moved to tears, remembering that here was one who had only been in a service once and had had no instruction. The Holy Spirit had taught her to pray. It was a solemn and holy moment and to cover our emotions we began to sing.

The words of familiar hymns were repeated and then sung together. The hour had grown late and we planned to make an early start for home next morning. Finally we said good night, but they just continued to sit. Finally one of the

One of the Last

young people asked, "Couldn't we sing just a few more hymns?"

Their desire was so obvious, how could we refuse them? So, tired as we were, we continued to teach them hymns and Bible verses. Finally they were willing to go back to their hut in the jungle, and we dropped into bed.

How wonderfully gracious is our heavenly Father! We had come to Acapulco to evangelize the troops but He had led us to camp within hearing distance of a lonely, fearful widow who was longing for God's blessing for her children. She was ignorant of Bible truths and only had a few distorted superstitions, gained through her half pagan village religion, yet Christ's love and compassion had broken through that night she heard the Gospel. God had become a reality to her and she wanted her children to share in the blessings she had experienced.

Early the next morning while we were closing and packing the trailer, the whole family came down to say goodbye and to thank us again for telling them of Christ.

"Sister, last night Sr. Huegel explained that God is our heavenly Father," I said to the old mother, "and that through Jesus Christ He has given you a new life. Now that new life has to grow and develop. You will need help in this and I am sure you will find it in that church you visited in Acapulco. I hope that all of you will try to go there each Sunday."

With her promise to attend the church ringing in our ears we pulled out of camp and watched them waving goodbye until, turning a corner, they were lost to sight.

A month and a half later I was back in La Caleta and had my family with me. We had come to enjoy a few days' vacation in that lovely spot. Almost immediately the women of the Indian family came to welcome us and we were delighted to learn that they had attended church on Sundays.

Soon the little Indian girl and our children were playing happily in the sand. What contrasts they made: our three tow-heads; our fair-skinned, red-headed; and the swarthy, black-haired child; chattering away in Spanish, all differences of race and background completely forgotten. Before our eyes was being enacted the truth of the beautiful hymn:
>In Christ there is no east or west,
>In Him no south or north,
>But one great fellowship of love
>Throughout the whole wide earth.

The week passed all too quickly and it came time for us to leave. The old mother came down to thank us again for coming.

"We had planned to send the boys over to the market and buy some shells for your children, but the restaurant has needed extra firewood and we could not make it," said the dear old soul. "You will be going right by the market as you drive into town. Would you stop and get some shells for the children?" And she pressed into my hand a fifty centavos piece.

"Oh, sister, I could not take this money! Thank you for the thought, but I know your boys only make four or five pesos a day from cutting wood from early morning until dark. It would not be right!"

"We all want to do this," she said, putting her hands behind her back to emphasize her refusal to take back the silver coin. "We want to do this for your children because you brought us the message about Christ."

It seemed almost like a modern "widow's mite" which I could not refuse. As we passed the market we bought the shells, and then with the children, prayed that God would multiply His blessing upon the whole family, and He did.

Five or six years passed. A friend and I were back in that coastal city. When we inquired about La Caleta we were told that it had changed completely. A hotel now stood upon the little island and bath houses and restaurants were numerous. Also, we were told that a colony of houses now occupied the area formerly covered with jungle.

We decided to drive out and satisfy our curiosity. When we reached it we could hardly believe our eyes. Everything had changed! It was completely commercialized. Gone was the lovely idyllic spot we had known. As we sat in the car, somewhat shocked by the complete change, a young man jumped on the running board.

"Would you like to go out in a boat on the bay?" he asked. "I have a very fine boat..." In surprise he stopped in mid sentence.

"Aren't you the man who some years ago brought us the Gospel?"

"Are you one of the family who had taken refuge in the jungle?" I inquired, almost more surprised than he. "Is your mother still living?"

"Yes, she is still here," he replied. "And I am her eldest son."

Then he quickly added, "Could you come and see us! We would all enjoy that, and also my youngest brother had an accident and is still in bed."

They had a nice little home and gave us a very warm welcome. They inqured for all my family and sent their good wishes. We were delighted to learn that they were regular attendants at the services in the little church in Acapulco.

One of the Last

By this time we were in the bedroom where the injured boy was lying. He had suffered a bad fall and they wanted to tell all the details because they felt that God had kept him from being killed. When they finished, we had prayer together thanking God for his goodness.

Then we had to hear all about the family. The boys had married and we met the wives. The Lord had prospered them and the boat was bringing in a good steady income. We were deeply moved by all we heard and in leaving felt constrained to again have prayer with the family, thanking God for guiding us to camp where we did on our first visit and for causing Fritz to pray in a loud voice so that the old mother could hear. How marvelous is God's providence!

Reluctantly we left the family and as we travelled we thanked God again for His goodness. We had come on the original visit for the purpose of evangelizing soldiers, but God also had in view this penniless, frightened widow whose only prayer was a heart's desire for God's blessing upon her family. It was unvoiced--but God heard as He has promised, "Before they call, I will answer." (Isaiah 65:24). And he caused us to camp within hearing distance of their hut. God had prospered them and the family had grown as the boys married. God's loving care was recognized and they were learning to lean on Him. All this because a faithful servant of God had been totally unconscious of his surroundings, as he poured out his heart before the One who loves to answer prayer, "Abundantly above that which we can ask or think." Truly great is God's faithfulness!

12

OTHERS JOIN IN THE ADVENTURE

The sky looked threatening and heavy clouds filled the horizon for the rainy season was due to begin any time now. However, it was too early to head home and so we decided to visit one more camp. Perhaps it might not rain today. We parked the car and began to climb the steep pathway that led to the outpost.

"Good afternoon, Sr. Taylor," said a cheery voice, and I looked up and saw a lieutenant standing above us. "It is good to see you again. Welcome to our camp." When we reached the top, he gave me a Mexican embrace and I introduced my companion.

"It is good to see you, too, lieutenant," I replied, but I could not recall his face nor his name, so I added, "Where did we meet last?"

"It is not surprising that you don't remember," he said, laughing heartily. "It is well over two years ago. I belong to the ninth regiment and you visited us on the Cuernavaca Road. You drew our attention to Christ's promise, 'I am come that they might have life, and that they may have it more abundantly.'" (John 10:10).

"You remember that verse!" I exclaimed.

"I not only memorized it, but I have proven it to be true. I accepted Christ, bought a Bible which I read each day, and He has changed my life completely." And he smiled broadly as he declared his faith.

"It is wonderful to hear you say that!"

"When I returned to camp about a week ago and learned that you had stopped here and had left literature, I was delighted and have been looking forward to your return."

Others Join in the Adventure 91

And then, without my having said anything about speaking, he called, "Sergeant, get all the men together, for I want them to hear Sr. Taylor's talk."

It was clear that the lieutenant remembered our routine and so I hung a chart on the side of one of the huts as the men began to gather. Just at that moment some peasants were passing along the road.

"*Señores, señores.*" shouted the lieutenant, and when he had their attention added, "I invite you to come up and join us while we listen to a talk about the love of God. It will be good news to each one of you. Come! You will be glad you did!"

Rather reluctantly the three men climbed the pathway to the camp and stood at some distance. However, as I began to point to things on the chart, they joined the group of soldiers. I had reached the point in my message where I began to prepare to give an invitation when the lieutenant asked to say something.

"I told you men to read the literature carefully because it told of Christ's love and could change your lives. It has changed mine completely!"

"*Señor,*" he said, addressing an old man who was among the peasants. "I see that you are prepared for rain and have your poncho with you. Please show it to me."

"My lieutenant, it is old and worn," protested the old man, "and is almost useless." And as he spoke, he unrolled the tattered rubber sheet so that we could all see that what he had said was true.

The lieutenant said a word to the sergeant, who went into one of the huts and in a moment returned and handed the lieutenant his own fine new poncho.

"These men have been telling you about the love of Christ. Some two years ago I heard this message and asked Christ to come into my life. He did and brought me a peace and joy I had never known before. Indeed he changed my life completely. To prove this, I want to give you my own poncho. Every time you use it I want you to remember the message you have heard today: Christ loves you and died for you." Then he passed the fine new poncho to the surprised old man.

The peasants were left almost speechless by the generosity of the officer, but finally found their voices. Profuse in their thanks, they went on their way assuring the lieutenant that they would remember the message. In their little village, I am sure that the officer's generosity must have been told and retold many times, and with it, we trust, the fact that it was the love of Christ in his heart which prompted this generous act.

This experience was just one of many which convinced us that when the seed is sown and we have done all we can to establish the faith of a convert, we can leave his nurture to God the Holy Spirit. He will lead him to the full stature of Christ. From time to time God gave us glimpses of what He was doing in the lives of the converts.

Such an experience came one day when I was at home because of my responsibilities in the seminary. We were just finishing lunch when the maid announced that a sergeant wanted to see me.

"Did he give his name?" I asked her.

"I think he said it was *Galvan*," she replied.

"Galvan!" I exclaimed. "It can't be possible. I have not heard from him for a year."

Galvan! What memories the name brought to mind. A weather-beaten hut, high in the mountains amid towering pines. A group of soldiers, muffled up in their *zarapes* against the chill wind, listening intently to the message. Finally, in response to the invitation, the raised hand of all the men, including thatof the sergeant. I remembered vividly his intense interest when I explained that God was ready to help in time of need, and his hesitancy when he asked if I would pray for his wife. He thought she had pneumonia! And at an altitude of over 10,000 feet!

I must confess that my faith began to falter as we walked toward the little hut. The room to which he led us was windowless, but as my eyes became accustomed to the darkness I could see that it was dirty and unkempt. On a heap of straw in a corner lay the sick woman, covered with a couple of threadbare blankets. Even with the door closed we still could feel the cold wind. We prayed for her and encouraged her husband to do so also. A couple of months later the sergeant and his wife came to my home to show how God had answered prayer...theirs as well as ours, I was glad to learn. She was the picture of health.

A few weeks later we had breakfast with them on another highway in a similar hut. But what a difference! The little hut was in order and spotlessly clean. The woman smiled contentedly as she sat beside the open fire preparing our breakfast. The sergeant, hovering near the fire ready to lend a hand, told us how Christ had changed their lives.

"I used to be loaded down with debts from gambling. Now I don't gamble and not a cent is owed to anyone." This was one of the changes that had come to them.

"He has stopped drinking," volunteered his wife.

Then as the meal was placed on a makeshift table, they stood together with bowed heads and tear-filled eyes as we thanked God for His goodness to them. Around the table we spoke of the need for daily Bible reading and prayer as basic for spiritual growth.

"I read a candle portion of the Bible each night," the sergeant volunteered.

"A what?" I exclaimed. And he, laughingly, told that each night he lighted a new candle and read his Bible until it burned out.

All these memories flooded my mind as I left the table and hurried out to the patio, anxious to hear all that had happened since I had last seen him. It was a joy to meet him again and find him still seeking to serve the Lord.

"God has been good to me," he said after he had greeted me with an unusually strong Mexican hug. "During the last months He has given me many opportunities to witness for Christ." He told of trying to win his comrades, of witnessing in some market places, and in the homes where he was billeted.

"But my happiest experience came after we moved from the north and I was stationed in a remote mountain village. My wife was not with me, so I was having my meals in one of the village homes. One day the father of the family died suddenly. When I heard the news, I hurried to the home and found the widow completely grief stricken. As I entered the room, the poor soul was kneeling at the foot of the bed caressing and kissing the feet of the dead man. 'These feet will never go again to help me collect firewood on the mountainside. They will never work in the fields again. I am alone! I am alone! Holy Mary, help me!'

"Lifting the poor woman, I placed her in a chair, and reading passages from the Bible, tried to comfort her. That afternoon I went with the family when they buried the old man.

"You know the custom, *senor*, of devout Roman Catholics is to have prayers for the dead for nine days after burial. That evening a crowd gathered at the widow's home for these prayers. After it was over, I arose and said I would like to read something which had brought peace and joy to my heart. Taking from my pocket 'The Way to God' by Moody, I read the first chapter. I did not read the chapter right through, but after each paragraph I took time to explain it carefully in order that all might understand. It took me over an hour, but the people listened eagerly. The first evening I brought two armed soldiers with me, just in case some fanatic might try to interfere. Instead of opposition, I found them eager to hear more.

"On subsequent nights, after the prayers were finished, I read other chapters. The interest was so great that I was asked to give two more *conferencias* in order to finish the book. This I did on the next two afternoons. I gave away all the literature I had and even lent my Bible. A few weeks later I was moved to another village, but have kept in touch with those people. A letter has come saying that some of these friends are coming to visit me in my new village to learn more about God. As soon as I received this message, I asked for special leave to go to the city to get more literature from you. My officer gave permission at once."

For a couple of hours we talked and prayed about the many opportunities to witness which God had given him. Then he left, carrying with him all the New Testaments, Gospel portions and tracts he felt he could use in the near future. He was proving himself to be a good soldier of Jesus Christ.

A few years passed, and then in 1938 he gave me the good news that he had been recommended to study in the Military College in Mexico City with the possibility of becoming a commissioned officer. Almost every week he would telephone with a word about his progress. The conversations would go something like this:

"Hello, Brother Taylor. This is Galvan speaking." And then he would inquire about my health and that of my family.

"How are you and how are your family?" I would reply.

"*Muy bien, gracias*. (Very well, thank you.) God is caring for them."

"And how are the studies progressing?" I would ask.

"They are hard, very hard, Brother Taylor. Keep on praying for me. God will see me through, I am sure."

"Yes, brother, we are remembering you," I would assure him. "And I know you are claiming the promise in God's Word, 'He has not given us the spirit of fear, but of love, power, and a sound mind.' (II Timothy 1:7). He will not fail you." And then would come a question or two about the soldier's work.

"Adios. Thank you for praying for me, *hermanito*." (Little brother--the diminutive is used as a term of affection.) Before I could answer, he had hung up.

Then came the day when he called and in his excitement he completely forgot all the polite preliminaries.

"Brother, God heard our prayers." His voice was vibrant with joy. "God heard and I have passed my examinations. They have recommended that I take more advanced courses!"

"I am so happy for you! Keep looking up, and God will see you through these new studies," I assured him. We

Others Join in the Adventure

talked for a much longer time than usual, mostly about how faithful God is and how He meets all our needs.

"Yes, indeed, brother, God is always faithful," he replied and then added, "but don't forget to continue to pray for me!" And as usual the click of the receiver being hung up drowned out my reply.

In earlier chapters, examples of God's guidance have been given which brought a thrill to our hearts. Sometimes the evidence of God's guidance only became clear after the occurrence but this, too, gave a feeling of assurance and thanksgiving. However, there is a special thrill when the guidance given one coincides perfectly with that which someone else has received, proving conclusively the providential working of the Lord.

A thrill of this kind came to Fritz and me on one of our visits to Acapulco. The officer commanding the zone had changed since our first visit to *El Fortin* with Curti's letter of introduction. The new commander gave permission to distribute literature but did not invite us to give a message. We were disappointed but grateful for the opportunity to reach a new group of soldiers.

When we finished distributing the Gospel portions at the hour of the evening roll call and were leaving the barracks, a sailor approached us and asked if he could have some literature.

"Have you visited the naval base across the bay?" he inquired. "There is a special concentration of naval personnel there right now."

"No, we have never been around there," I answered.

"It is just a short distance around the bay, and there is a road all the way," he volunteered, giving a few more details of where to find it.

There was still at least an hour of daylight, and if it was so close, perhaps we might find the commander in his office and get permission to give the men the literature at morning roll call. It was worth trying, because the next day we had to return to Mexico City.

Following the sailor's instructions, we picked up the road around the bay, but it was soon clear that the sailor must have come from the naval base by boat and not by road. As we progressed, it became increasingly bad. Pothole after pothole was encountered until we wondered whether we would have any springs on the car for our trip home.

Our speed was reduced to a crawl. The sun set and, as happens in the tropics, the darkness came down like a curtain. It was completely dark when we reached a large closed gate and our headlights centered on a big sign. "Absolutely no admittance." While sitting there wondering what to do, and asking for God's guidance, the answer came in the form of a five-year-old boy who climbed on the running board to get my attention. He was stark naked!

"For five centavos, I'll open the gate for you," he offered.

"But it says, 'Absolutely no admittance,'" I answered.

"Everybody just drives through!" was his prompt reply.

Clutching the five centavos in his fist, he climbed the large woven wire gate, reached over to unlatch it, and riding the gate he swung into the darkness, and we drove through.

We had not gone far before we were challenged and the guard told us to stay where we were while he brought an officer. In a few moments a very pleasant young officer appeared and asked why we had come. Experience taught us that it was unwise to tell our business to junior officers; the higher the rank, the less likelihood of a turn-down.

"I would like to see the commander, if it is possible at this late hour," I explained.

He ushered us into a very pleasant waiting room. The moon had just come up and through the cluster of palm trees we could see several naval vessels at anchor in the bay. In a few minutes the officer was back. He evidently had a good sense of humor, because very seriously, but with a twinkle in his eye, he informed us, "The commander regrets that he cannot receive you....He is in his bath!" We joined him in a good laugh, and the ice being broken, he inquired why we wanted to see the commander.

"Please tell the commander that this afternoon we distributed this literature to all the soldiers in *El Fortin*. A sailor who was watching suggested that we might give the same literature to the naval personnel. We do not want to overlook anyone and would be glad to do so here if it could be done in the morning. We must return to Mexico City tomorrow."

We gave the young officer samples of the Gospel portions for the men and the New Testaments we would give to the officers. In a few moments he was back with instructions for us to be there at nine in the morning. With thankful hearts but without realizing yet how wonderfully God had worked, we crawled back over the potholes to Acapulco.

The next morning the same courteous young officer met us and presented us to the commander. He welcomed us in perfect English and chatted for a few minutes about what we had done among the military. Then he led us to the parade ground, where all the men of the naval base were lined up. Quickly we went down the ranks giving the men Gospel portions and New Testaments to the officers. Then the

Others Join in the Adventure

commander explained that not all the officers were present and so he led us to their homes and saw that each had a New Testament. Also he asked for literature for all the men who were on duty on the vessels in the harbor.

"It may interest you to know why I was so anxious that my men have these portions of God's Word," he said as we walked to our car. "I am a graduate of a mission school in Mexico and of a Lutheran college in the States. I have my own Bible and read it daily. Since taking command here, I have been wondering what I could do for the spiritual welfare of my men. Then you appear with your kind offer to give my men portions of God's Word."

Then followed sincere thanks for our thoughtfulness in responding to the suggestion of the sailor at the barracks. A man who reads his Bible daily will in all probability be a man who prays. I feel sure that his "wondering" what he could do for his men was done with God. God in His providence had that sailor at the barracks. I do not know how often God uses naked urchins to further His plan, but I am sure that, without the boy's confident, "Everybody just drives through," we might well have turned back and would have missed seeing God answer that commander's deep desire for his men.

In an earlier chapter I referred to Christ's own words, "He that followeth me shall not walk in darkness, but shall have the light of life." (John 8:12). This promise hinges on obedience. Immediately it raises the question: how much must a man understand about the Bible truths before he can follow Christ? He said, "He that cometh unto me, I will in no wise cast out." (John 6:37). From the following story told by one soldier, it would seem the heart's desire rather than head knowledge is what counts.

A new battalion was on the highway, and as was customary, on our second visit the chart of the Two Ways was hung on the side of a hut and the soldiers were invited to listen to an explanation of the literature left with them a week before. Ten or twelve soldiers gathered around and one of them seemed especially interested. He stood nearer than the others and occasionally nodded his head in assent to something that had been said. When the invitation was given, he was one of the first to raise his hand. When the message was finished he immediately came to me.

"Sr. Taylor, for years I have believed in Christ but today for the first time I have understood what He did for us all when He died on the cross." He smiled at my exclamation of surprise that he could have believed without understanding.

"In my little mountain village the priest used to invite us all to gather in the shade at the back of the church after mass. There he would read to us the story of Jesus from the Bible. Hearing of the miracles that Jesus did, the people He healed, and the love He showed in people, made a deep impression on me. The priest would say, 'It is Christ you need, not Mary.'"

"Then I joined the army and in the *Cristero* revolution I was severely wounded in one of the battles. The Federal forces were driven back and had to leave their wounded. The *Cristeros* found me and chopped me up with their machetes."

As he said this, he pulled up his shirt, showing a chest and stomach that were a mass of scars.

"All night long I lay in mud made from my own blood. In my intense agony I was conscious of a presence near me. I cannot describe it more than that I was not alone. I had cried out to God and God was near.

"In the morning the Federal troops drove the *Cristeros* back. A medical officer came and looked at me and then moved on. 'Doctor, help me,' I cried in desperation. 'I know I am going to live. I know I am going to live.' In response to my cries he returned and did what he could for me and then called the stretcher bearers. In the field hospital they stitched up wound after wound. I was in the hospital a very long time and had a number of operations, but look at me now. I am as strong as any of the men. Jesus was with me that night and He healed me. Of this I am sure. I am so thankful that now I understand what He did for me when He died on the cross."

I was deeply touched by the dear boy's testimony and thankful I could add a word of explanation to the teaching of that unknown village priest who, for his love of Christ and compassion for his people, had the courage to speak against a Roman dogma and tell the people that Christ was the One they really needed!

After working for a year or two among the Mexican military it was not uncommon for us to be greeted like this when we visited a new unit: "We wondered when you would get to us. So-and-so in such-and-such regiment told us about your visits. When will you come back and show us a chart?"

To the men who opened their hearts to Christ He became a living reality. Their lives were changed, they were experiencing the "more abundant" life which He had promised and they wanted to tell others about it. Like the early Christians, they could not keep silent. In all probability they had never heard Christ's words, "You shall be witnesses unto Me," but the Holy Spirit guided them to tell others. Without realizing it, they were joining the multitude who over the centuries and around the world have felt the urge to adventure with God, having experienced his love and power.

13

A WAY IN THE WILDERNESS

"God was with us on this trip to Veracruz," I said to Geraldine as I dropped my bag in the hall. "It is good to be home, but, having driven all day, I am tired and hungry."

"Supper will be ready by the time you have washed up. At the table I want to hear all about the trip."

I had left four days before to drive three Mission Board members to Veracruz. On the way down, we had visited several churches, an army camp or two, and the second day they had taken a plane to Yucatan. The following day was a national holiday with its usual parade. I had planned to try and obtain permission to distribute literature to the troops taking part in this celebration in Veracruz. It had been some years since this military zone had been visited.

"The plane was two hours late in leaving and, by the time I reached army headquarters, the general and all the senior officers had left. The sentry told me that the general would not be back at the headquarters the next day because he had to be on the reviewing stand in the center of the city. Very much discouraged, I returned to the car and sat there asking the Lord where we had gone wrong in planning. I had felt definitely that this was an opportunity I should not miss.

"Suddenly I was aware that a car was pulling up at the entrance and two officers got out. In a moment I was out of my car and the sentry, anticipating my question, called out, 'You're in luck. That was the general. He must have forgotten something!' I spoke to the general as he returned to the car and permission was given at once.

A Way in the Wilderness

"Then I drove to the church to tell the Rev. Placido Lope that all was arranged. I had seen him earlier when the group visited his church and he had agreed to help in the literature distribution next day if permission were given. He was very interested to hear how God had brought the general back to his office at just the right moment. When he saw how eagerly the soldiers received the literature and the response of a group in a camp near the city, he summed up his impression by saying, 'This has thrilled me. There is no doubt God is working.'"

"This experience reminds me of how you and Mr. Brown were guided when you went to the barracks on Monterey."

"You mean when the officer of the guard turned out to be a member of the First Baptist Church of Mexico City?"

"Yes! On that occasion the providence of God was clearly seen."

"You are right! If the young officer had not recognized the Gospel portions we had in our hands, we would have gone into the main office and would have been turned down by an antagonistic colonel. He showed us how to get to see the general by entering through a back door."

"These experiences of God's guidance help me in my praying when you are away on trips," Geraldine added.

"And your 'expecting' to see God work strengthens our faith, dear," I replied.

"I almost forgot to tell you, Cam Townsend called today and wants you to get in touch with him as soon as possible," Geraldine said. When we left the table I telephoned him.

"Hello, Cam. Geraldine said that you wanted me to call as soon as I got back. What's new?"

"Two things," Cam replied, "and both are of interest to you. A few weeks ago General Cardenas took command of the Pacific Coast military zone. Since Pearl Harbor there has been a concentration of troops in Lower California to discourage any attempt on the part of the Japanese to land troops there and attack California. Today I received a letter from the general inviting me to visit him in Ensenada when I go to the west coast in a couple of weeks. I thought you might like to come along and try to secure permission from him to visit those troops? We are driving and there is room for you in the car."

"It would be a great opportunity, Cam, and I would like to go with you if I can arrange for my seminary classes. When do you plan to leave?"

"I hope to leave two weeks from next Thursday."

"I will begin to work on the matter at once and will let you know as soon as possible. If the general will give permission, it will mean returning there for two or three months to do the job properly."

"I would plan on that, but you can be back from this preliminary visit in ten days."

The appeal was almost irresistible and I felt inclined to accept at once but Geraldine advised against it. It had been our custom for years when seeking God's guidance to ask Him to confirm it by giving us a Bible promise. She saw no reason for not doing so in this case. Within a few days we had the promise, "I will do a new thing....I will make a way in the wilderness and rivers in the desert." (Isaiah 43:19). It seemed amazingly appropriate because at that time much of Lower California was a wilderness and sparsely populated. Through the Holy Spirit we believed that streams of Living Water could flow there.

Meanwhile Cam had received another letter from General Cardenas saying that we were to be his guests at a certain motel in Ensenada. So on the date planned we were on our way, going first to Cam's old home in Santa Ana to leave Mrs. Townsend. Then he and I drove to the General's headquarters in Lower California. After registering at the motel, Cam went to army headquarters to greet the general. In a short time he was back with the good news that in the afternoon we were to have tea at the Cardenas' home, where he would discuss with me the details of my proposed visit.

"Cam, it looks as though his permission is assured!" I exclaimed excitedly.

"I did not have any doubt about the permission being given," he replied. "The general has known for years of the work that you have been doing among the troops."

When we met in the afternoon, the general was very cordial and began to explain the condition of the roads I would have to traverse.

"It will be impossible for you to use an ordinary car. They do not have enough clearance for that kind of road. Actually, many of them are just trails across the desert," he added.

"What I am using for this work is a half-ton truck with a station wagon body on it," I replied.

"In that case, I think you can get down to most of the camps." And then he changed the subject, saying, "Please do not confine your work to the troops alone, but give your message to the civilians as well. They are isolated and need God's truth." There was a note in his voice that surprised me. It almost seemed to be one of yearning. Then I recalled that here was a man who, as president of the republic, had been known for his interest in the Indians and the humble people of his country. Evidently he still felt a burden for them.

"It will be impossible for me to give you an official pass, Sr. Taylor, but I will send word to the commanders of the zones and you will have no difficulties. Let me have some of your literature, and I will send it to them. Then they will recognize you when you appear. Report at my headquarters when you come back for the three month visit."

After we left the general's home, Cam drove south for a short distance and soon we were convinced that the general's estimate of the roads had not been exaggerated. They were trails, not roads!

The general had suggested that we would enjoy knowing a Russian family who lived in Ensenada, and so we called on Mr. and Mrs. Federenko and found them to be deeply dedicated Christians. To our surprise, they told us that at least once a week and sometimes oftener General Cardenas would come to their home about nine o'clock at night and would ask Mrs. Federenko to play hymns on their little folding organ. He would join in the singing.

"Sra. Federenko, what kind of hymns does he like?" I inquired.

"Señor, he likes the *triste* (solemn) ones and not the ones that are *alegre*."

"Give me an example or two, please," I asked, and from these it became clear that he wanted hymns with content in the words rather than just choruses.

Later, on my return, I became better acquainted with the Federenkos and found them to be not only dedicated Christians but most interesting people. One thing I will always remember was the very original way they protected their large strawberry patch from birds. Almost half an acre was planted in rows, but every fifteen feet there was a wider path. Along these paths were strung heavy wires which were fastened to stout posts at each end. They had several cats and each day borrowed others from their neighbors. On the cats were placed collars with short cords which were tied to large rings on the wires. The cats ran freely back and forth on the pathways and few birds sampled the Federenkos' strawberries.

From Ensenada we headed back to California and I returned to Mexico City by air. In our conversation the general had mentioned repeatedly how isolated were the camps; that there were very few villages and no means of amusement. He suggested that, in addition to a projector to show Bible slides, I try to bring a movie projector and films of a general character. The movie projector would have to run on 12-volt batteries. In Los Angeles I was told that such a projector would have to be ordered specially. They agreed that this type of machine probably could be found in Mexico City rather than in the States. This made me optimistic, because the manager of Eastman Kodak was a friend. Immediately upon my return I went to see him and explained what I needed.

"Norm, if you had come a week ago, I could have fixed you up at once. We ordered several of the movie projectors which run on batteries, but to our surprise they did not sell as we had expected. Just last week I sent the last one to the shop to be rewired, and I am afraid that they will have begun work on it. If they have not, I can give it to you at a discount; what it would have cost to rewire it."

He picked up his phone and dialed a number. "What have you done on that 12-volt projector we sent out last week?" he inquired, and I listened eagerly to the one-sided conversation. "No! I am not asking how soon you can get the work done. Have you started work on it? I have a purchaser for a 12-volt machine." After he got a reply, he said, "Good! Then send it back to the store." Turning to me, he said, "The projector is yours. You can pick it up tomorrow."

In my reading I had come across another promise which was claimed for this venture. It was a free translation of Proverbs 4:12, "When thou goest the way shall open up before thee step by step." This accurately describes what happened as preparations were made. Extra funds were received, slides on the life of Christ and even movie films were loaned. But the most remarkable evidence of God working out our problems was seen in the way I obtained a new set of tires.

Because of the war and the scarcity of raw materials, tires in Mexico were being rationed. Several dealers told me that it was hopeless for me to apply for new tires and that all I could do was to have the old ones retreaded. However, they were old and in bad condition. Even when retreaded, they could not take the roads in Lower California.

Before this problem, we just tried to lean a little harder on the new promise. Then someone reminded me that the manager of the Goodrich Tire Company was a member of Union Church. I went to see him, and explained the reason for this trip and my need for new tires.

"I am sorry, Taylor, but we are bound by the government regulations just as the agents are, and could not sell you any of our regular tires without authorization."

A Way in the Wilderness

"Then the only thing I can do is to have the old ones retreaded, but my experience with retreads has not been encouraging."

My disappointment must have shown in my voice, for he immediately continued. "There is another possibility. We have 'seconds' which for some minor defect have been rejected. I could have the foreman pick out four on which the defect is so minor that it will not affect the mileage you get from them, and, of course, the price is much less than the cost of new ones. My own car is equipped with them."

It only took a few minutes to pay for the tires and arrange to have them put on the carryall the next day. When I returned home and Geraldine saw my face, she exclaimed, "You got the tires!"

"Yes!" I exclaimed happily, "our God is the God of the impossible. I got tires and the price was only about half what I had expected." Together we thanked the Lord for supplying this most important item of equipment for the trip.

Over the years many people had helped in the work among the soldiers. Some, like Fritz Huegel, had done so on a systematic basis, giving one day or more a week. Among these was an elder in the local church, Sr. Hilario Llopis. He had a store and while he was helping me his wife took care of the business. After he had done this voluntarily for a number of months, we put it on a business basis. Therefore, when I was thinking of someone to accompany me, he seemed the logical person to invite. He accepted and proved most helpful on the trip. His ability to deal with people was unusual.

At last our expedition was ready and we set out on the long drive north and across the continent. To accommodate the large amount of literature and equipment, long boxes had been installed on each side of the carryall and these served as bunks for us at night. After we crossed the border, we found that a 35-mile-an-hour speed limit was being enforced to save on gasoline consumption, and so we drove 24 hours each day. One slept while the other drove.

Soon we reached Tijuana, the gateway to Lower California. We were so anxious to begin work that we decided to go to a barracks there before reporting to General Cardenas in Ensenada. If God had not intervened, our enthusiasm might have caused us real trouble.

We arrived at the barracks when the men were forming ranks for their morning roll call. A major was on the parade ground and we went to him immediately.

"Good morning, major. General Cardenas has given permission for us to distribute this literature to the troops in the Pacific Coast military zones." And I passed him a Gospel portion and a New Testament.

"Religious literature!" he exclaimed in surprise.

"Yes, they are part of the Bible," I answered. "We have distributed this literature to troops in many parts of the republic and General Cardenas has invited us to do so here."

"We have received no such orders and while I am in command here, no one is going to give my men this kind of religious propaganda. Anyone doing it should be arrested."

While we were speaking, an air force captain had ridden into the square on a motorcycle and had come over to where we were standing. He heard our conversation.

"I assure you this has been thoroughly discussed with General Cardenas and he..." The captain interrupted me.

"Major, I would be careful not to jump to conclusions. I saw this man in Mexico City giving out this same literature to all the troops before the parade on the sixteenth of September. The top brass were there and knew what was being done. I have no doubt that General Cardenas knows about this. Somehow you must have failed to get his order." The major was in an awkward position and obviously was in a quandary as to what he should do.

"Major, you were right in refusing when you had not received any orders, and I congratulate you on your carefulness," I volunteered. "If you wish, we will return later when we are sure you have received the proper order."

"Oh, no!" he replied. "I take the captain's and your word that this is on the level. You can give the men these booklets right now."

As we drove away from the barracks, we thanked God for the providential arrival of the captain. Otherwise we might have ended up being arrested by the angry major. In view of this experience, we thought it prudent to report to General Cardenas before visiting any other troops.

On the way to Ensenada we reviewed how God had guided in recent weeks. His promise was that "The way shall open up...step by step." He had fulfilled that promise in supplying all the equipment needed. Had this morning been a "step" or a misstep? We were not sure, but we had seen God work and could go forward with greater faith and expectancy.

14

STREAMS IN THE DESERT

"Welcome to Lower California," said General Cardenas when I was ushered into his office. "Are you all prepared to visit the outposts?"

"Yes, general, and as you suggested, I have brought along a movie projector as well as one for the Bible scenes."

"Good. All the commanders have been advised of your coming and you will be welcomed in the camps and villages. Don't forget to include the civilian population when you are in the villages." He made a few comments about the conditions of the roads, wished us a successful trip, and then, rising from his desk, shook hands and walked with me to the door. He was a very busy man and I appreciated the time he had given me. I joined Llopis in the truck.

"The general wished us a good trip. I feel he wants us to get to the outposts as soon as possible, so let us just distribute the literature in the barracks here. We can preach when we return from the south if there is an opportunity. We know from experience that our best work can be done in the camps."

Literature was distributed in the barracks and by early afternoon we were on our way south. The sky was clear and the day beautiful. On our right we caught glimpses of the ocean and on the left were the foothills, rising into blue distant mountains. Soon the paved road changed to gravel. Before long it ended and we were on the roads of which the general had spoken.

"Brother, if this is the kind of road we will have to travel over, my teeth will be jarred loose long before we reach home!" I said laughingly to Llopis.

"If we don't get many far worse than this, I will be happy," he replied. He was right. These trails were good compared to those we encountered in the mountainous regions, where we frequently had to stop and remove rocks before proceeding. Often we had to travel at a crawl to avoid breaking a spring. In open areas the trails multiplied, the drivers having found it easier to break new ones rather than contend with the ruts and dust of the main trail.

"Brother Taylor, you run the projectors each night and let me explain the Bible picture," Llopis said to me as we drove along. "I know nothing about projectors and if anything went wrong, I doubt if I could fix it."

"You are right," I replied. "And furthermore, it is much better that you, a Mexican, should give the first conference rather than a foreigner." I was glad that he had volunteered, because he had a gift for speaking and as the weeks went by, he became really eloquent when describing the Bible scenes. We continued to bump along the trail.

"Let's learn from others and make our own trail," I suggested, and we got some relief from the dust but our speed was reduced.

The sun was getting low when in the distance we saw a house or two and hoped we were nearing the first village, Santo Tomas. Ahead was a soldier walking along the road and we stopped as we reached him.

"*Senor*, where will we find the officer who commands this outpost?"

"If you will give me a lift, I will show you his house," and he jumped in the front seat beside us.

"It's the house over there," he said as we entered the village and then volunteered, "Drive right across the field to the house." We did as he suggested.

As he left us I said, "Tell all your friends and the people of the village that tonight we hope to show movies and still pictures, if the colonel will give permission." His exclamation of pleasure at the prospect showed how really isolated they were. We pulled up in front of the house he had indicated and, before we could leave the car, two officers came out to greet us.

"Colonel, I am Norman Taylor, at your orders, and this is my friend, Hilario Llopis. I received permission from General Cardenas to visit the outposts. We come equipped to show movies and still pictures at night and, to add to the entertainment, there will be music from the radio and phonograph."

"You are more than welcome! We received word of your coming a week or two ago. Perhaps the town square will be the best place to put on the show and you can camp right there, too. I will send a soldier to show you the place. How long can you stay?"

"Two nights," I replied. "We want to touch as many outposts as possible and we don't have a large repertoire. However, we are keeping in reserve one set of pictures to show when we return here."

Soon we were in the village square and pulled into a large open space between two houses. The screen for the pictures was put in place with guy ropes fastened to tent pegs to hold it steady should it become windy. We hardly had time to eat before the crowd began to gather. Then we backed the carryall out, opened the tailgate, and I set up the projectors, using the ends of the lockers in the car as stands. Music was already being played and the crowd clustered around, watching all that was going on inside the carryall.

When it was dark enough, we showed a movie of a rodeo which delighted the crowd. In those early days there were no sound tracks on the films, but no commentary was needed for that type. When we changed to still Bible pictures, Sr. Llopis explained them as we progressed. While the movie of the rodeo was being shown, the crowd had laughed a great deal and made audible comments. But after one or two Bible slides they became very quiet and reverent.

As we finished the last picture, Sr. Llopis announced, "We have little booklets, part of the Holy Bible, which relate in detail the story you have just seen in the pictures. We will give a copy to anyone who will promise to read it carefully."

Hands went up everywhere and he returned to the truck to get the Gospel portions and began to distribute them to the crowd who pressed around him.

I turned off the projector and joined him in the distribution. It was a very orderly crowd and we were touched by their profuse thanks and their reiterated promise to read the booklet carefully. Soon they disappeared in the darkness and we climbed into our sleeping bags.

"It is time to get up. There are several people around the truck," said Llopis as he awakened me early the next morning. "They want to hear more. I'll take a chart and talk to them while you get some breakfast. Then you can relieve me."

"Okay!" I replied. "It is hardly daylight. Imagine their coming this early."

As I prepared a hurried breakfast the crowd grew, and by the time I had eaten and had tidied up the carryall, Llopis had finished his message from the first chart. I took over and began to explain the chart a second time. Some of the original group stayed on and others kept coming. For most of the day we kept explaining the Way of Salvation to eager listeners.

On the second night the crowd was even larger and we learned that some civilians had ridden long distances to attend. To gather the crowd, a travelogue was shown first and then the second series on the Life of Christ. As scenes of the crucifixion were shown, there was a silence which could almost be felt.

"It was the love of God for each one of us that brought Jesus Christ to the cross," said Llopis. "For God so loved the world, and everyone in it, that He gave His only begotten son that whosoever believes in Him will not perish but have everlasting life." After a pause he added, "If any of you wish to understand more clearly what Jesus Christ did for us when he died on the cross, come back here tomorrow morning. Remember that our eternal destiny depends on our attitude toward Christ." Recalling how early people had come that morning he added, "Come at about seven o'clock. We must leave by ten to go on to the next outpost."

By sunrise people had begun to gather again and then we learned that few had watches and time was referred to by the position of the sun. We hung charts on both sides of the car. Those who had heard the first one were encouraged to go to the other side and hear a new message, "The Three Crosses." To use their terminology, the sun was past "midheaven" before we could leave.

As we went from one place to another, these scenes were repeated night after night. Often in isolated outposts only the soldiers, fifteen or twenty, and their families were present. However, as news of our coming spread, civilians seemed to appear from nowhere.

After about five weeks, we reached El Rosario, two hundred and fifty miles south of the border. It was larger than any of the communities we had visited. We arrived there about noon. Soon all arrangements had been made with the commander, General Moreno. In the afternoon we decided to visit all the homes, leave a Gospel portion and invite the people to the evening program. We had hardly started before we were stopped.

Streams in the Desert

"What kind of propaganda are you distributing? It must stop at once. It is against the law!" The speaker identified himself as the village constable.

"*Señor*, we are here at the personal invitation of General Cardenas, the ex-president of Mexico. I am sure you must be mistaken when you say this is against the law. General Cardenas would not have asked us to break the law of the republic."

"Have you anything to show that the general gave you permission?"

"No, we don't. But General Moreno was advised of our coming."

"I will have to take you to see the mayor," said the policeman. He realized that he was getting into deep water and this seemed an easy way out. Poor fellow, he did not realize that he was only getting in deeper than ever.

"Señor mayor, I found these men distributing religious propaganda to the homes in the village. They say that General Cardenas gave them permission, but have nothing to prove it."

"Oh *señores*, welcome to El Rosario. General Moreno told me of your gracious offer to show pictures in the village square tonight. We are very grateful to you for coming." Then he turned to the policeman.

"Juan, go with the *señores* and help them, so that they will not miss any of the homes of our people."

As we left the mayor, we could see that the poor policeman was very embarrassed, and to try to set him at ease we commended him on his thoughtful vigilance for the welfare of the villagers. After he had accompanied us to a number of homes, I thanked him for the help he had given.

"Don Juan, I am sure that you have many duties to attend to and we can locate the remaining homes. Thank you for your help and we will see you this evening when we show the pictures. Your presence at that time will be really useful." We shook hands and he left us.

That night the village square was filled with people, more than we had considered possible in such a sparsely populated area. Then we learned that many men had ridden from distant points because the next day was Sunday and all men of military age had to come for several hours of military training. Our friend the constable was very much in evidence and seemed eager to tell everyone that he was associated with us in the program.

As in other places, the people were delighted with the movie of the rodeo. The still pictures of the Life of Christ left them deeply impressed and they eagerly asked for more. They had been so quiet and reverent as they watched that I could not resist putting on some extra slides that would not detract from the second series, which were to be shown the following night.

As I shut off the projector, Mr. Llopis announced, "Today we left portions of the Holy Bible in all the homes in El Rosario. However, we understand that some of you are from outside of town and to you we will give these booklets right now." As the people began to crowd around us, he added, "For those who would like to hear more of God's Word, we will give a conference tomorrow morning when the sun is clear above the eastern mountains." We had learned from our experience in Santo Tomas their customary way of announcing the hour for anything special.

Shortly after sunrise, a good group had gathered and while Sr. Llopis spoke to them, I decided to take a walk around the village. At a distance I could see a large number of men drilling under the command of an officer we had met the night before. I was curious and approached the group. When I neared them, to my great surprise I heard the command to the marching men: "Halt! Stand at ease!" And the officer left his men and came over to me.

"Sr. Taylor, many of these men heard the program last night and would like to know more. Could you give them a conference when they finish drilling?"

"Lieutenant, I will be delighted to do this. At what hour will you be through with their training?"

"We will be finished at eleven o'clock." He had a watch!

"All right. When they are finished, let them gather at the side of that hut and I will be here with a chart which will help them understand."

"I know that it will be a great help. Some years ago I heard you speak, using a chart, and it made things very clear. We were on one of the highways near Mexico City."

"You did!" I exclaimed in surprise. "And you remember the message?"

"Of course, but I want to hear it again and I am staying for the lecture."

Leaving the officer and men to continue their drilling, I returned to the truck and watched the large crowd that had gathered around Llopis. They were very interested and there was a good response when he gave the invitation.

"Brother Llopis, before you lose this growd, why not offer to explain the chart of the Three Crosses. I have the opportunity to speak to the men who are drilling and had better use the chart you have just finished." Following my suggestion, he spoke to the crowd.

Streams in the Desert

"If you are interested, I could give you another conference right now which will help you understand even more clearly what Jesus Christ did for all of us when He died on the Cross. How many of you will stay?"

"Yes, do give us more teaching," several replied, and most raised their hands signifying that they would remain.

One added in a loud voice. "This is Sunday and we don't have to work. Go ahead, we want to know more."

Llopis changed the charts and passed the one he had been using to me. I stood in the background and was delighted to notice that most of the people stayed to listen to the second message.

Right at eleven o'clock the lieutenant dismissed the men and about seventy-five came over to where I had hung the chart. They listened intently while I explained the Way of Salvation. As these men had not had time to read the Gospels we had given out the night before, I was sure they had questions and asked that they express them.

"It seems too easy, just believing," said one man.

"It was not easy for the Lord Jesus Christ. Think of what he suffered on the cross. We all have sinned and rebelled against God. We deserve to be punished, but the Holy Scripture says, 'The Lord laid upon Him the iniquity of us all,' (Isaiah 53:6) and in another place Saint Peter tells us, 'Who His own self bare our sins in His own body on the tree that we, being dead to sin, might live unto righteousness; by whose stripes we are healed.'" (1 Peter 2:24).

"How could the death of one man free us all from punishment?"

"Look who that man was! He was God! God will judge everyone someday and now He is giving us the chance to repent and believe the Good News that Jesus died for all. If we reject Him, what will our fate be in the Day of Judgment? There was nothing greater that God could do to show His love for us than to suffer and die in our place."

"How good God is!" exclaimed one man audibly.

"Jesus gave us an invitation. You can read it in the eleventh chapter of the booklets we gave you last night, 'Come unto me, all ye that labor and are heavy laden and I will give you rest.' (Matthew 11:28). What will be your response to this invitation given by the Lord Jesus Christ?"

Almost all signified their desire to follow Christ. They seemed deeply touched and very sincere in their decisions.

"Jesus said, 'To as many as received Him to them He gave the right to become the sons of God' (John 1:12) and in another place He said, 'I am come that they may have life and have it more abundantly.' (John 10:10). He has given you a new life. It must grow, so read God's Word. Remember you are sons of God and He wants you to tell Him your needs. He promises to answer. I have heard hundreds of soldiers tell how God has heard and answered their prayers. He will do the same for you.

"If any of you would like to have a Bible or New Testament, we have them in the truck and the price is quite low," I added as the group broke up.

I returned to the truck and a large number of men followed me to buy Bibles or New Testaments. Many decided to stay in town for the evening program and in the afternoon groups could be seen sitting in the shade reading God's Word.

The evening meeting was something to remember for a long time. There was no moon and no clouds in the sky, and so the stars seemed to shine like a million diamonds in their canopy of blackness. In front of us was the brightly lit screen, showing the vivid colors of the Bible pictures. In the shadows we could see dozens of people seated on the ground listening, with rapt attention, as the story in pictures unfolded. As on other nights, the silence was profound when we reached the scenes of the Last Supper, in the garden, Christ's betrayal, and the crucifixion. As the last picture blacked out, the impression was so profound that Sr. Llopis waited several minutes before breaking the silence. Then he reminded the people that after the sun had risen the next day we would continue to explain with charts the blessings that God has for all who follow Christ.

The next day we pulled out of El Rosario after spending several hours dealing with the groups which came to listen to further messages from the charts. From the very first night on this trip we had been conscious that the Spirit of God had worked in each village and camp, but in a very special way, "Streams of Living Water" flowed in the desert in El Rosario. God was fulfilling the promise He had given us.

As we continued southward, the roads became even worse than they had been. Now there were bridgeless gullies to cross that were difficult to maneuver because of the length of the carryall. Evidently the vehicles used by the military were jeeps or short-bodied trucks. On one occasion we were trying to cross a narrow gulch when the rear end of the carryall scraped along the ground as the front wheels began to climb the opposite side. We found ourselves suspended between the two banks and the rear wheels revolving

uselessly in the air. To free ourselves, we had to jack up
first one side and then the other to put rocks under the
rear wheels. After several hours of work, we extricated
ourselves and were happy to reach the army camp without
further problems.

This outpost was on the seashore and as we approached
and felt the cool sea breeze, we exclaimed about how good
it was after the heat inland. We could look forward to a
sound sleep that night!

Our welcome by the soldiers was as warm and cordial as
usual and as it grew dark, they and their families gathered
around the carryall to listen to the music. This always
gave us an opportunity to get acquainted. We noted that no
civilians were present, but sometime while the pictures
were being shown, a hard-boiled customer with two big guns
on his belt joined the group.

When the Bible pictures were finished and we began to
give Bible portions to the people, he asked for a copy and
then at first opportunity approached Llopis.

"*Senor*, may I speak to you privately?" he asked.

"Of course," replied Llopis. "Let's go over to the
shore." And they went behind the carryall and sat down on
some rocks.

The soldiers did not want to leave and I continued to
answer questions about the pictures they had seen. They
were very interested. Finally they all left and I was able
to crawl into my sleeping bag and, enjoying the cool ocean
breeze, dozed off at once.

An hour or two later I awoke and became conscious of the
murmur of voices. Raising myself on my elbow, I could see
Hilario and the stranger still talking earnestly. Bits of
their conversation reached me. "There are no sins that
Jesus Christ will not forgive..." It was Hilario's voice.

"But surely he..." and after the first exclamation the
stranger's words did not reach me.

"The Bible says, 'Though your sins are as scarlet they
shall be white as snow' and you..." Hilario's voice low-
ered and I lost the rest of the sentence.

"You remember what the Lord's Prayer says? Forgive us
our sins as we forgive those that sin against us."

The stranger's answer did not reach me, so I dropped
back on my pillow and asked the Lord to open his understanding and his heart. In a moment I was asleep again.
Sometime later, I felt the carryall shake and was conscious
of my companion lying down on his bunk. At sunrise, as we
were eating breakfast, he gave me some of the details.

"I have never met anyone so full of hate. He was on his
way to murder a man in Tijuana....Yes, he finally accepted

the Lord and asked Him to cleanse his heart and forgive him. I believe he is sincere, but we must continually pray for him. Only God can keep that hate from returning if he begins to think of his grievances again."

"That day the officer commanding the zone came through in a jeep. When he heard of the difficulty we had had getting across the gully on the road to this camp, he strongly recommended that we should not try to visit the outposts farther on.

"If you had difficulty in crossing the dry stream bed just north of this camp," he said, "you will never be able to cross the gulches farther on. The hills come down close to the coast and so the streams have no chance to spread out as they do in the plains. I strongly recommend that you do not try to go farther. If you would care to give me the literature for the men in these camps, I will see that it is distributed."

"General, we are grateful to you for your advice," I replied, "and if you will be so kind as to see that the men get the literature, we will not go any farther."

As we returned to the camps we had visited on our way down, it thrilled us to find that the converts were following the routine we had recommended.

"How many of you are reading a portion of God's Word each day?" I asked in almost every camp, and was pleased to see that many were doing so. Some said that they were finding their reading not only interesting but very helpful. One man's remark was echoed by others.

"In some places it almost seems as though God is speaking to me personally."

"That is what He wants to do. Remember He is your heavenly Father and you are His sons. Expect Him to speak to you and He will not disappoint you," I answered.

To help them to grow spiritually, we tried to get the name of a civilian in each village and promised to send Sunday School literature from time to time. We suggested that they meet in groups to study it together.

After a couple of weeks, we were back in El Rosario and called on General Moreno. We had chatted for a little while about our experiences in the various camps. Then suddenly his tone changed, but he had a twinkle in his eye.

He said reprovingly, "How do you men explain your failure to visit San Quintin on your way down? The general told you to visit all the camps."

"Did we miss an outpost?" I inquired laughingly.

"You did, indeed! But the thing that surprised us is that you missed only this one."

"Is it north or south of El Rosario?" I inquired.

"Fortunately, it is north and you can make a visit as you return to Ensenada," the general replied. "San Quentin is on the coastal plain. An old flour mill is located there and we have a large detachment of soldiers because of the fine harbor on which it is located. The main trail passes a large clump of juniper trees. After you pass them, turn toward the coast. There will be marks from the trucks; follow them."

When we reached the area indicated, we began to look for the trees. Finally we spotted some that seemed to fit the description, but from them trails seemed to run in every direction. The first try ended in a salt marsh. The second and third try were equally fruitless. Llopis was driving and was trying to find his way up a rather steep sand dune.

"Stop!" I exclaimed. "Look at what is ahead of us!"

"It is not possible! We must be seeing things!" he responded.

Such a reaction was not surprising, because there in the desert, right in front of us, was an old cemetery. The fence was broken down and the headstones all awry. Judging from the number of headstones, at one time there must have been quite a large village nearby. As we looked toward the shore, we could see where the village had been, for scattered through the sagebrush were old foundations and footings where the houses had stood. On the beach and into the water were rotten wooden piles, showing that at one time a quay had stretched out into the bay.

But where was the outpost? In the gathering dusk we saw a building around the bay and, skirting a salt marsh, we finally reached the spot and found it to be the old mill, with the outpost close by.

"Good evening," a lieutenant greeted us. "Can we serve you in any way?"

"At the invitation of General Cardenas we are visiting the outposts and missed you when coming down."

"Oh, you are the *senores* who have put on the shows in the other camps. We have heard about you. Welcome to San Quintin."

"It is getting dark. Where would you suggest that we set up the screen for the pictures?"

"Since there will be a full moon tonight, I think it might be well to put it inside the entrance to the old warehouse," he replied.

Then we noticed an old warehouse which jutted out into the bay. It looked about ready to collapse, for the piles were rotten and, although the roof seemed intact, sections of the walls were missing.

"Don't drive inside! It might fall down. Park just at the entrance and put the screen inside."

This we did, and grabbed a bite of supper before the soldiers and their families began to appear. The lieutenant was one of the first and inquired whether we needed any further help.

"Lieutenant, this place intrigues me. What is its history?"

"Before the First World War, there was quite a town here. On the plateaus in the hills a lot of wheat was grown and an English company built this flour mill. It was operated by the rise and fall of the tide, which at this point is quite high. And also there is this fine harbor. As the war continued, coastline vessels stopped touching here and the population gradually drifted away when there was no sale for their grain."

"That is understandable, but why did the village disappear and the mill and warehouse remain?" I inquired.

"That is easily explained," he said with an amused smile. "The mill was taken by the government for nonpayment of taxes, and a guard was stationed here. After the war, coastline vessels came into the harbor, pulled down enough houses to give them a load, and sold the materials anywhere they could."

We had placed the truck on a narrow strip of land which gave access to the warehouse, backing in in order to use the lockers as stands for the projectors. The music was started as we made final preparations and the soldiers and their families gathered round, most of them sitting on the floor of the old warehouse.

Soon the show was in progress, beginning with the movie of the rodeo. As usual, this delighted the crowd. The still pictures of Bible scenes left them deeply touched, as they had in all the camps. After we had given out Gospel portions to all, we announced that in the morning we would explain the pictures more fully with the use of illustrated charts.

"In the other camps you explained several charts. Give us one tonight. We want to see everything that you showed in other places."

They were so eager to hear more that we could not deny them and I hung the chart of the Two Ways on the side wall of the old warehouse. I wanted to turn the car around and get the headlights on the chart, but the strip of land was too narrow and we found it was impossible.

The problem was solved when from somewhere an old smoky oil lamp appeared and a barrel was rolled into place under the chart. With the lamp on it, the details of the chart could be seen fairly clearly.

The scene was unforgettable! Gaping holes in the warehouse walls framed a moonlit sea and in the distance great white waves broke on the rocks at the entrance into the bay. Near at hand, the rising tide poured with a steady roar through the broken sluice gates into the bay beyond. Before me were the eager faces of my listeners. Some were silhouetted against the gaping holes in the walls. The faces of those near at hand could be seen dimly in the light of the lamp. Forgotten was the late hour, and the strange surroundings, as I saw their eager faces and rapt attention as they listened to the old, old story of God's love and goodness.

An hour passed and the heads of the little children were resting on their mothers' shoulders or knees, but the older children and the adults still listened intently as questions were asked and points clarified. It was clear that they had heard a lot about our visits in other camps. At last I inquired what their response was to Christ's invitation. It seemed to be unanimous. If the attendance and the interest shown at the meeting next day were any indication, their decisions were genuine. So great was the interest that the lieutenant cancelled most of the daily routine to allow the men to attend the meetings.

"Rivers" really flowed in the desert during the two days we remained at San Quintin.

On the morning of the third day we left there. We had shown them all our pictures and explained all the charts. So they had seen everything used in the other camps.

Travelling northward, the remaining camps were revisited and the converts encouraged in their Christian faith. It was about the end of the twelfth week when we reached Ensenada. In the barracks there, it seemed impossible to get the men together for a conference, they were kept so busy. And so we had to be satisfied with giving the men another Gospel portion.

General Cardenas was out of town, so I reported to one of his aides that we were returning to Mexico City. Then we called on the Federencos to say goodbye.

We left for home with joyful hearts. God had fulfilled His promise! He had made a Way in the Wilderness and we had seen streams of Living Water flow in the desert.

We were so thrilled by all that we had experience that the long drive home to Mexico City seemed no hardship. We were also looking forward with keen interest to seeing our friends in the army outposts again, and in learning how they were progressing in their Christian walk. It was well that we could not see into the future!

15

DISAPPOINTMENT OR HIS APPOINTMENT?

Immediately upon our return from Lower California we began again to visit the army camps on the highways near Mexico City. It was a joy to find that the men had continued to read their Bibles and to pray. There was clear evidence of spiritual growth. For some time we had been using a new chart illustrating "The Vine and the Branches" (John 15) to teach the truth of our union with Christ. Many had discovered that the promise of Christ's constant presence brought a feeling of security and joy.

We had learned that a positive message brought the most lasting results and so never referred to differences between the Catholic and Protestant churches. We had enough in common upon which to build true Christian faith. When questions arose, we tried to help the believer find the answer in the Bible. Usually, this was sufficient.

One day we visited a camp where most of the soldiers had been believers for several years. The conference was finished and we were preparing to leave when the wife of the corporal stopped me. She carried her baby in her arms.

"*Señor* Taylor, may I speak to you?" she asked, and we walked aside from the group.

"What is your problem?" I inquired. I clearly recalled that both she and her husband had made professions of faith a year or two before.

"Would you do me a favor?" she asked. As I agreed at once, she continued, "When you are in the center of the city and near the shops, will you please buy me a little image of Christ?"

"Did not you and your husband make professions of faith in Christ some time ago?" I asked when I had recovered from my surprise.

"Oh, yes, at Tres Cumbres."

"Why then do you want a little figure of Christ?"

"I think it will help me to realize that Christ is with me."

I did not want to hurt the dear woman's feelings, and silently asked the Lord to help me. I think He did!

"Señora, your baby is very sweet. Let me have her and I will give you a photograph of her which you could put on the wall and you would not have to carry her."

"No-o-o!" and she looked at me as though she thought I was crazy. "I want my baby!"

"Christ promised, 'Lo I am with you always,' and 'I will never leave you nor forsake you.' When you have Christ Himself in your heart, why would you want a little image? Don't you believe that He will do what He has promised?"

"Oh yes!" she answered, and after a few moments of thought she added, "It would be wrong?"

"I would rather say that it is unnecessary. Just as the picture of your baby is unnecessary when you have her in your arms."

"Of course!" she replied. "I know He is in my heart and can be more real to me than a little image." And her face lit up with a happy smile.

I left the camp thankful for another example of how living and real Christ can become to one who believes the promises of His constant presence.

Several months passed, and one day I dropped into the office of a friend who represented an American Christian organization.

"I am so glad you came in," he said after greeting me. "I have a big surprise for you!" As I had no idea to what he referred, I remained silent. "I have reported your evangelistic work among the Mexican soldiers to our home office. They are very interested, and, I believe, are going to give enough New Testaments so that every soldier can have his own copy."

"That is very kind of them," I finally said. Sheer surprise had left me almost speechless. "How soon will they come?" After a few more words of thanks, I left. As I drove home, I tried to analyze my lack of enthusiasm and felt just a little ashamed. When I reached home, I told Geraldine about the offer and my failure to be profuse in my thanks.

"Perhaps you feel that way because experience has taught you that Bibles and New Testaments given to converts are not appreciated and taken care of as those for which some nominal price has been paid."

"You may be right," I replied. "Over the years we have found that to be true, and have not given anything larger than a Gospel portion. However, I must recognize that this gift of New Testaments was not solicited. God may have some special purpose in sending it at this time." A couple of weeks later the offer was confirmed by my friend.

"Norm, a letter today says that the printing of the New Testaments has begun and they will have to know at once the total number needed."

"We will have to get that information at the military headquarters, so I will come downtown at once. How soon can we expect the books to be shipped? It will take me over two months to make the distribution country-wide."

"In less than three months, I expect," my friend replied.

"Good! I will be at your office in less than an hour."

Our friend at the headquarters was very interested when we explained the object of our visit. He suggested a dedicatory inscription to put on the front of the New Testaments and at our request wrote it out for us. We received the needed information and thanked him for his help. We had not gone far when my friend stopped.

"I should have asked the general for a letter acknowledging our gift of the New Testaments," he said.

"A what?" I exclaimed, and he repeated what he had said. "You will never get anything in writing from anyone in authority. I know this situation, having worked in it for thirteen years. I have never received anything in writing. No passes! Nothing! They have let me work freely, but if there should be a reaction, no one is personally responsible. Please explain the situation to your office."

A stalemate seemed to have developed. The New Testaments had arrived, but the donors had not given permission for them to be distributed. I was given a sample by my friend, but nothing more. After some weeks of uncertainty a telephone call caused me to hurry to my friend's office.

"I guess you were right," he said as he greeted me. "We cannot get any kind of official acknowledgment. Since so much time has been lost, we have decided to make the distribution through the local Protestant churches in other parts of the country. You do it in the Federal District and in Cuernavaca..."

"If you are going to do it in that way, please impress upon the pastors the need to make the distribution as unobtrusively as possible and without any publicity. Don't even announce it in the churches. If it is publicized, we could have trouble."

My friend agreed to this and showed me the circular letter he had written to the pastors. He asked them to form committees to do the distributing. This was to be done on a certain date, making it simultaneous in all parts of the country. He agreed that I should begin at once in the local outposts. I did so in the Federal District, but before I could get to Cuernavaca, our world caved in.

In a coastal city, a pastor showed the letter to the editor of a very liberal newspaper and he published it before the date set for the distribution. In the next issue of the Catholic weekly, the military headquarters was denounced for having agreed to the distribution and the various commanders for having allowed Protestant work to be done among the troops. The next edition continued the attack and carried pictures of the New Testaments showing the designation, *"Edicion Militar."*

Immediately following this second attack an aide to the general brought a verbal message to me: "Stop all visits to army outposts." Even now there was nothing in writing! I had hoped that the furor might pass, but after some weeks, when I tried to visit one of the outposts where everyone knew me, the officer very regretfully refused me admittance. The order was to be strictly enforced.

To me, who had given so many years to this work and loved it, the closing of the outposts came as a terrific shock. To my repeated "Why, Lord?" He helped me to see that a subtle change had come which I had failed to recognize. In view of this, the work might have ended in a short time anyway. The war in Europe had brought a Mexican version of the draft. No longer were the army recruits from the rural areas and often semi-literate. Now they came from cities and towns. I had not encountered them in the camps because they were still undergoing training in the barracks.

I began to see that I should be grateful for the timing of the distribution of the New Testaments. If I had tried to do it all, taking some months to complete the work, I might not have had time. Word of the distribution would have reached the hierarchy and it would have been stopped. By having it done simultaneously, many men received New Testaments who would not have if my plan had been followed. So, in my disappointment, I could see God working for good. (Romans 8:28).

Some four months prior to these events my two young sons, Leigh and Norman, had been very seriously injured in an accident. Both suffered fractured skulls. One was unconscious for six days, the other for ten. After weeks in

Disappointment or His Appointment? 125

hospitals, we were able to bring them home to convalesce. By early summer they were able to be up and around, but the doctors refused to allow them to return to school. It was felt that another month or two of inactivity was needed. When the Mission Board learned this, they advised that we take a furlough. This would allow the boys to start school afresh in September. The Mexican school year corresponded to the calendar year.

Even before leaving for our furlough, Geraldine and I, in our prayer time together, were feeling the lack of definite information about the needs of the soldiers. We found that we were having to pray in general terms. As we drove northward, we saw many soldiers patrolling the highway. We stopped to say goodbye to those we knew and were delighted to find that many had their New Testaments in their pockets and assured us they were continuing to study them. This was a great encouragement to continue to pray that they develop spiritually.

We had reached California and were comfortable settled in an apartment in Pasadena when one day Geraldine came into the room and exclaimed excitedly, "You have been troubled about having to pray in general terms for the soldiers. Listen to what has come to me as I read Romans 8, verses 26 and 27, 'We do not know how to pray as we ought...The Spirit intercedes...according to the will of God.' You see what this promises? We pray in general terms to the best of our knowledge and the Spirit takes those prayers and applies them as He sees the need!"

"I believe you have touched on the secret of successful praying, dear! Why haven't I seen that before? That is the lesson I should have learned from my experience with Van Slyke and the church prayer calendar." And we reminded each other of what had happened more than ten years earlier.

The Van Slykes, who labored for many years among the Zapotec Indians in Oaxaca, had been transferred to Mexico City. We had called to welcome them. In the course of our visit, Van inquired about the work among the soldiers and added, "Norm, I am very anxious to go with you on the highway and see something of the work you are doing."

"I would be delighted to have you come any time. It so happens that I have no companion for next Thursday. Could you make it?"

He accepted and I picked him up early that day. We went to the Cuernavaca Highway and had a wonderful time. There were larger groups in the camps than usual and they were very responsive. After hearing me explain the chart a couple of times, Van asked to take his turn in giving the message. That day thirty-nine soldiers made decisions for

Christ. And most of them bought Bibles or New Testaments. We were having such a time of blessing that we continued to visit camps until it began to get dark. Reluctantly we started for home.

"Norm, do you always have a response such as we have seen today?" Van asked.

"No, indeed! Today was something special and I can't account for it."

As we drove along, we continued to speak about how remarkably God had worked and the evidence of the Holy Spirit in the hearts of the men. We rounded a bend in the road. Suddenly we saw the whole of the Anahuac Valley spread out before us and the lights of Mexico City like a million diamonds below us. At that very moment a thought came to my mind.

"Van, I believe that this is the day that our names appear in our denomination's prayer calendar. Do you recall our date?"

"No, I don't," he replied, "but you may be right."

"Think of what this proves. Thousands of our church members may have prayed nothing more than, 'Lord bless the Van Slykes and the Taylors,' but God took those prayers and applied them to the need of the moment, and thirty-nine men accepted Christ."

When we reached home, I hurred to my study and picked up the Year Book of Prayer. There were our names on the list for that day.

"How in the world did we miss the deeper lesson in this experience?" I repeated to Geraldine after we had recalled the incident.

"It shows that God always has a fresh truth for us to learn," she responded, "and I am thankful He brought this fact to me this morning. Now we can pray with greater assurance."

During our furlough I visited churches in many states and frequently ended my message with this story. People told me that it encouraged them to use the prayer calendar more faithfully and to remember that God has promised to answer every prayer that is offered. His answer may be a yes, a no, or wait; but He does answer.

As our furlough progressed, we constantly sought the Lord for guidance as to our future missionary work. During the previous decade and a half God had marvellously fulfilled the promise He had given, "I will bring the blind by a way that they knew not..." (Isaiah 42:16). Every detail of the promise had been fulfilled beyond our highest expectations. As we thought and prayed about the future, it suddenly came to me that the last phrase of the promise, "These things I

Disappointment or His Appointment?

will do unto them and not forsake them," gave the assurance of God's continued presence and guidance. So we claimed the promise afresh for the future.

About a month before our furlough was to end, a letter came from the Mission Board. I opened it and read the contents with a feeling of growing wonder.

"Geraldine, where are you?" I called, and hearing her voice from the kitchen hurried there. "Here is the answer to our prayers!" I said as I passed the letter to her. As she read the letter, her face broke into a broad smile.

"Isn't God wonderful! Again He has answered 'abundantly above all we could ask or think.' This appointment makes Latin America our field of service!"

"That is true, but what thrills me most about this appointment is that it is something absolutely new. We have never had this kind of an organization in our area before."

"Then our old and proven promise in Isaiah 42 is applicable in this case," Geraldine exclaimed. "The work will be 'paths that we have not known,' and we have the assurance, 'These things I will do unto them and not forsake them.'"

"It is great to have such a word of assurance before taking up a new responsibility. It gives me a wonderful feeling of confidence. I am convinced that God will guide."

The letter had brought the news that the Mission Board had appointed me chairman of the newly formed Latin American Council, composed of mission representatives from the six countries in which our denomination was working. We had met in Guatemala a few weeks before to complete the organization and anything which would develop a closer relationship between the fields was within the scope of its activities.

A survey of the fields and consultation with missionaries and nationals made it clear that certain projects should be begun without delay. Returning from this trip I was able to report:

> The opportunities are almost limitless. To bring the fields closer together, there is no better way than to get them praying for each other. So my first project is to start a prayer bulletin. Also, the requests for evangelistic campaigns, Bible conferences, and retreats are so numerous that we will need more than one evangelist. As a starter, I am going to contact Ramon Cabrera, who used to broadcast through HCJB in Quito, Ecuador, and see whether he would be interested in becoming our evangelist....

Soon the Prayer Bulletin was going out monthly and carried prayer requests from all over Latin America. Each month tracts were sent to all pastors and workers and, as anticipated, one evangelist was unable to respond to all the invitations our office received. To meet this need we were led to begin something completely new: the interchange of national pastors between fields. Outstanding pastors were invited to donate their vacations and go to some other country to hold four special meetings. God used this to create bonds of friendship between churches in different lands.

The guidance of the Spirit was sought in the development of all projects and confirming promises were received. Isaiah 42:16 was again the basis for our expectations. With a slight change in the form of the organization, this work continued for another thirteen years. For eight years careful statistics were kept. During that period over one hundred special meetings were held annually in the six countries. In these eight years, thirteen million tracts were sent to the churches for distribution. It was thrilling to see God work in so many and varied ways. Our missionary service continued to be an adventure.

Because my responsibilities were administrative, no longer could I be on the scene where the activities were taking place. However, through our prayers, we joined our colleagues who were doing the work. We never were able to know exactly the special needs of each campaign, but we could pray for them with confidence remembering the promise found in Romans 8: "We know not what we should pray for as we ought...but the Spirit maketh intercession for us according to the will of God." Thus we could rejoice with them in all that God was doing through their ministries.

Recalling the lesson learned so many years before from a study of the parable of the Sower, we could in faith anticipate and thank God for the harvest that is assured when the Seed is sown. "But others fell on good ground and brought forth fruit, some an hundredfold, some sixtyfold and some thirtyfold." Results could be expected since they are clearly promised.

Occasionally I had the thrill of being with my associates when the providence of God was clearly seen. Such an experience occurred on a visit to Brazil. The missionaries in the state of Matto Grosso had met in Buriti for a regional meeting. Buriti is situated at the geographical center of South America.

When the gathering concluded, the pilot of the mission plane ferried the visitors to Cuiaba, the capitol of the state, from where they could get transportation back to

Disappointment or His Appointment?

their respective fields. When this was completed, three of us adults and two children were to be flown to Rio Verde, about three hours away by air.

The ferrying took longer than anticipated and it was quite late in the afternoon when we took off. After we had been in the air for a short time, I noticed with some apprehension that the sun was getting very low in the west.

"Can we possibly make Rio Verde before dark?" I asked George Glass, the pilot.

"We won't have much light to spare when we reach there," he replied. He was English and I recognized it as a typical understatement. A few minutes later, feeling perhaps that something further was needed, he added, "It will be dark long before we reach Rio Verde, but in the hinterland there is an unwritten law that if a plane circles a town after dark, someone will come out in a car and shine the headlights down the airstrip. In these places there are no landing lights."

After the sunset, I had never seen anything so black as the ground beneath us. There was no way of telling whether we were flying over jungle or plain.

"George, you are flying by compass and there is a side wind; in the dark, no landmarks are visible. What navigation system do you have?" I inquired.

"Just dead reckoning," he laughed, "but I allow a little for the side wind. However, the town is on a river and if we miss it, we only have to fly up or down the river until we see its lights. We will not miss it by much," he said confidently.

At last the lights of the town became visible and I congratulated George on his good navigation. Soon we were over the town and began to circle. All of us looked eagerly for a car heading out toward the landing strip. Several cars moved about, but none left the streets of the town. Later we learned that the local pilot had been practicing landing the night before and everyone thought he was continuing to do so a second night. Actually, he was out of town.

We continued to circle. Five minutes passed, ten, fifteen, twenty—and still no sign of help. By this time, all of us realized that something had gone wrong. The others were praying, I am sure, as I was. There came to mind the promise that had meant so much to me while flying in France, "The eternal God is thy refuge..." and I put us all in His hands.

"I guess we will have to get down by ourselves," said George. "Our gas is getting low."

"Can you find the strip in the dark?" I asked.

"Yes," he replied. "There is a shed at one end and it has a tin roof which will show up in the darkness." What he did not tell us was that he was not sure of the direction the strip went from the shed. Obviously this was vital. One more circle of the town and we headed out into the darkness.

"Thank the Lord for His help!" George exclaimed when he sighted the hut on the airstrip, for right in front of it was a parked DC3, whose whiteness showed up clearly in the dark.

"They always park facing down the airstrip. Although we cannot see it, the narrow strip has to be in that direction. And the ground is about six feet under the tip of the DC3's wing."

Coming in for a landing, he flew directly toward the tip of the right wing, side-slipped a little, and tucked the left wing of our little plane under the right wing of the DC3. We touched the ground and rolled to a stop.

With hearts full of gratitude to God for His providence in having the DC3 on the landing strip, we climbed out of our cramped positions in the little plane. Suddenly it seemed that the darkness had disappeared. The heavens were full of stars and light, as were our hearts as we trudged the mile into town.

How wonderfully faithful is our God! He is able and ready to meet our every need. Over the years this conviction had been growing as hundreds of promises were fulfilled under so many varied circumstances. Now it had become a certainty: God's promises could not fail! Concerning this, He Himself had said, "God is not a man, that He should lie; neither the son of man, that He should repent: hath He not said, and shall He not do it? Hath He not spoken, and shall He not make it good?" (Numbers 23:19).

16

SUNSET GLOW

As I come to the end of this narrative of God's goodness in fulfilling, even to the smallest detail, the promises given in His Word, I would echo the praise of the Psalmist: "Bless the Lord, O my soul, and all that is within me, bless His Holy Name." (Psalm 103:1)

Seeing God fulfill His promises not only strengthened my faith, but transformed my ministry into an adventure with God. The spirit of expectancy which it created has not only kept me young in spirit, but, I believe, has contributed toward my good health. This was true in the life of Caleb. As he waited with keen anticipation for the fulfillment of Moses' promise of an inheritance, he was able to say to Joshua, "I am this day four score and five years old, yet I am strong....Give me this mountain, whereof the Lord spoke in that day....And Joshua blessed him and gave unto Caleb...Hebron for an inheritance." (Joshua 14). A spirit of expectancy did keep Caleb young!

I stated in my introduction that God has given a promise for every need which can arise in life. With equal assurance I might have said also that there is a promise for every stage of life: from childhood to old age. The latter caught my attention when, after thirty-six years of service, I retired from foreigh mission work. Opportunities came to serve in churches at home and, for this new kind of service, a promise found in the Psalms was claimed. "The righteous shall floruish like palm trees...that flourish in the temple of our God, that still bring forth fruit in old age." (Psalm 92:12, TEV). Such a promise encouraged one to expect results!

After retiring, I was reviewing past years and found that, by a strange coincidence, my Christian service, from my call into the ministry until retirement, was divided into three periods of thirteen years each. To me then, thirteen was not an unlucky number but the very opposite--a number of blessing. And why not? At the table during the Last Supper were the twelve apostles and the Lord Jesus. Then the thirteenth person was Christ, not Judas. Thirteen meant to them the Presence of the very Son of God!

In 1972, at eighty and after another thirteen years serving in various churches, I felt led to retire from that work, but not from the Lord's service! Again I sought the Lord for His promises for the last period of life. I found them in Joel's propnecy, which was quoted by Peter in his message on the Day of Pentecost. "I will pour out my Spirit on all flesh . . . your old men shall dream dreams, your young men shall see visions." (Joel 2:28). Dream dreams of what kind? Dreams of an expectant heart to see this prophecy fulfilled in the pouring out of His Spirit all around the world. Truly a second Pentecost!

Thank God for imagination! By it we can roam the world through prayer. No Iron or Bamboo Curtain can shut us out. No physical handicap need halt our travels. The world is our field and the opportunities are limitless.

It was our pleasure to welcome to Mexico and into our home the first five Wycliffe Bible Translators. As the number grew, we continued to follow them with great interest, praying for them in their isolated tribes that God's presence might surround them, and that Divine wisdom might be given for the problems of translation. Now (1985), although there are over five thousand five hundred translators scattered around the world, they are still within easy reach. The Lord Himself promised, "Whatsoever you ask in My Name, that will I do, that the Father may be glorified in the Son" (John 14:13). He will be glorified as millions who have never heard, find Him through new translations! Why not travel widely through prayer!

Also, it can be a joy to follow in imagination the many messages that go out over the airwaves through radio and television. Tens of thousands are touched each day in this way. What a privilege to speed our prayers through these open doors, asking that God's Word may prove to be "Quick and powerful . . . the discerner of the thoughts and intents of the heart" (Hebrews 4:12). And also, "That it shall not return void" (Isaiah 55:11). Every Christian broadcaster continually asks that his messages be followed in this way!

And if ill health keeps you from church, try being present in spirit. Your prayers might change your church and transform your minister's preaching. You could be the unknown one who is holding up his hands—unknown to him, perhaps, but known to God.

And, although we will not know here and now the results of our praying, this activity can create in our hearts and minds a spirit of expectancy which will bring to pass for us that marvelous promise, "The path of the just (justified) is as a shining light that shineth more and more unto the perfect day." (Proverbs 4:18). That day when we shall awake with His likeness! (Psalm 17:15).

God's promises cannot fail!

HELPS FOR DAILY LIVING

A classified list of Bible promises mentioned in this book and others used to meet problems and needs under varied circumstances.

WHY WERE THESE BIBLE PROMISES GIVEN?

1. To encourage us to come to God in prayer.
2. To make Christ a living reality. When God speaks note the personal pronouns used. This makes them very intimate and real!
3. To Strengthen our faith by creating a feeling of expectancy.
4. To make our Christian faith practical for daily living.

HOW CAN THESE PROMISES BE USED MOST EFFECTIVELY?

1. As a reason for praise and thanksgiving, as well as a basis for petitions, in our daily devotions.
2. To help confirm divine guidance. Ask for and seek a Bible promise.
3. In faith claim the promise and anticipate its fulfillment with thanksgiving and praise.
4. When reading the Bible look for promises, underline them and keep a list for future use.

PROVEN PROMISES

ABIDING. Psalm 91:9-12; John 14:23; John 15:5-7, 10; John 17:20-26; 2 Corinthians 6:16.

AFFLICTIONS. Psalm 34:19; Isaiah 43:2; 2 Corinthians 1:4; 2 Corinthians 4:16-18; Hebrews 4:15-16; James 5:13-15.

ANXIETY. Psalm 27:1; Psalm 34:17; Proverbs 16:3; Isaiah 26:3; Philippians 4:6-7; 1 Peter 5:7.

ASSURANCE. John 3:36; John 5:24; John 6:37; John 10:28-30; John 14:12-14.

BURDENS. Matthew 11:28-30; 1 Peter 5:7.

CHRIST (Death of-). John 3:16; 1 Peter 2:24

CHRIST (Power of-). 1 Corinthians 15:57; 2 Corinthians 2:14; Philippians 4:13; 1 Peter 5:10-11; 1 John 5:4-5.

CHRIST (Presence of-). Matthew 28:20; John 14:18-21; 2 Corinthians 4:6; Ephesians 3:17-19; Hebrews 13:5.

CLEANSING. Isaiah 1:18; Ezekial 11:19-20; John 15:3; Hebrews 9:13-14; 1 John 1:7-9

COMFORT. Psalm 23:4; Psalm 147:3; Isaiah 66:13; John 14:16, 18; 2 Corinthians 1:3-5.

COMMITMENT. Psalm 37:4-5; Matthew 28:18-20; John 1:12-13; John 6:37; Hebrews 12:1-2.

DEATH. Psalm 23:4; Isaiah 25:8; 1 Corinthians 15:54-57; Revelations 21:4.

ETERNAL LIFE. John 3:36; John 5:24; John 10:27-29; Romans 6:23.

FAITH. Isaiah 26:3-4; Hebrews 11:1.

FORGIVENESS. Psalm 103:12; Isaiah 1:18; Isaiah 44:22; Matthew 6:14-15.

FRUIT BEARING. John 14:12-13; John 15:5, 8, 16.

GOD (Our Heavenly Father) Psalm 103:13; John 1:12; John 16:23-24; 2 Corinthians 6:18; Ephesians 4:6; James 1:17-18.

GOD (His Loving Care) Psalm 23:1-6; Psalm 34:7; Psalm 91; Psalm 121; Isaiah 35:3-4; John 10:11-16.

GUIDANCE. Psalm 32:8; Psalm 37:23; Proverbs 4:11-12; Isaiah 30:21; Isaiah 42:16; Isaiah 43:19; Matthew 4:19.

HOLY SPIRIT. Ezekial 36:27; Joel 2:28-29; Luke 11:13; John 14:16-17; John 16:13-15; Romans 8:26-27; Galatians 5:22-25.

LIFE ABUNDANT. Psalm 16:11; Psalm 36:7-9; John 6:35, 37; John 10:10; Romans 6:4.

LIGHT (Divine). Proverbs 4:18; Isaiah 60:19-20; John 8:12; John 9:5; 2 Corinthians 4:6.

LOVE (Divine). Deuteronomy 7:9; Proverbs 8:17; Isaiah 38:17; Jeremiah 31:3; John 3:16; John 17:23-26; Romans 5:5-8; Romans 8:35-39; Ephesians 2:4-7.

LOVE (Toward God). Psalm 91:14-16; John 14:21-24; I Corinthians 2:9-10; I Corinthians 13:1-13; Ephesians 3:16-21; 1 John 4:8-12.

OLD AGE. Joshua 14:12-13; Psalm 92:12, 14 (TEV); Joel 2:28; Acts 2:17.

PEACE. Psalm 37:11; Isaiah 26:3; Luke 1:79; John 14:27; John 16:33; Romans 15:13.

PRAISE. Psalm 50:23; Psalm 147:1; Isaiah 43:21; Hebrews 13:15; 1 Peter 2:9.

PROMISES (Of God). Numbers 23:19; Psalm 119:162 (TEV); 2 Peter 3:8-9.

HELP FOR DAILY LIVING

PRAYER. Psalm 4:3; Psalm 34:15; Psalm 66:18-20; Isaiah 40:28-31; Isaiah 58:9-10; Isaiah 65:24; Jeremiah 33:3; John 14:13-14; John 15:7 and 16; John 16:23-24; Romans 8:26-27; James 5:15-16; 1 John 5:14-15.

PROTECTION. Deuteronomy 33:27; Psalm 34:7; Psalm 91:1; Psalm 121:5; Nahum 1:7; 2 Timothy 4:18.

PROVIDENCE. Psalm 32:7; Psalm 37:28; Psalm 41:1-2; Psalm 107:7-8; Romans 8:28; 2 Timothy 4:18.

SUFFERING (Chastening). Job 5:17; Proverbs 3:11-12; Hebrews 12:7, 9-11; 1 Peter 1:5-9.

SALVATION. Psalm 50:23 (TEV); Isaiah 53:5-6; Zephaniah 3:17; John 3:15-17; John 6:37; Acts 16:31; Titus 3:3-7; Hebrews 9:28; 1 Peter 2:24-25; Revelation 22:17

TESTING. 2 Corinthians 10:3-5; Ephesians 6:12-13; Hebrews 12:12; 1 Peter 1:6-7; 1 Peter 4:12-13.

THANKSGIVING. Psalm 26:7; Psalm 95:2; Philippians 4:6-7.

TROUBLES (all kinds). Psalms 34:7 & 17; 37:39-40; 46:1; 91:2-3, 14, 15; Isaiah 43:2; Joel 2:32; 2 Timothy 4:18.

WISDOM. Psalm 19:7; Proverbs 2:1-12; Provergs 3:13-18, 21-26, 35; Proverbs 8:11-12; Daniel 12:3; James 1:5.

WORD OF GOD. Isaiah 55:11; Matthew 13:2-9; 18-23; Hebrews 4:12.